Cpt. Jose 'Pepi' Granado is a graduate of St. Thomas University. He's a retired captain with 35 years of law enforcement experience spanning two agencies, Miami Police Department for 25 years and Miami Gardens Police Department for 11 years. During his illustrious career, he investigated and managed over 800 homicide and death investigations. As a subject matter expert, his experience and leadership allowed for his ascension to captain overseeing the Criminal Investigations Division. Throughout his career, he was instrumental in establishing investigative protocols, and training/mentoring inexperienced investigators and supervisors. He is devoted to teach a new generation of investigators. May this book be used as a guide for those who wish to expand their knowledge in the criminal investigations or criminal justice field.

This book is dedicated to those who inspired me in one way or another. To my wife, Lissette, and to all my children and grandchildren, from whom I draw continuous energy. To my friends (Mike, Milly, and Patrick) who encouraged me throughout this venture. To my late mother, Bertina, who was a consummate fighter, my brother Carlos, and to my late father, Armando Granado. A special appreciation to the City of Miami Police Department, Miami Gardens Police Department and to all of my colleagues and 'team' members. I, especially, wish to praise the Almighty, whose guidance has sustained me through personal and professional situations.

Cpt. Jose 'Pepi' Granado

THE HOMICIDE MANIFESTO

PROTOCOLS OF A VIOLENT CRIME'S INVESTIGATION

To Willy
The Best Attorney
and Great Friend...
Cpt "Pepi"

AUSTIN MACAULEY PUBLISHERS™
LONDON • CAMBRIDGE • NEW YORK • SHARJAH

Austin Macauley is committed to publishing works of quality and integrity. In this spirit, we are proud to offer this book to our readers; however, the story, the experiences, and the words are the author's alone.

Ordering Information:
Quantity sales: special discounts are available on quantity purchases by corporations, associations, and others. For details, contact the publisher at the address below.

Publisher's Cataloging-in-Publication data
Granado, Cpt. Jose 'Pepi'
The Homicide Manifesto

ISBN 9781643787428 (Paperback)
ISBN 9781643787435 (Hardback)
ISBN 9781645365037 (ePub e-book)

Library of Congress Control Number: 2020900729

www.austinmacauley.com/us

First Published (2020)
Austin Macauley Publishers LLC
40 Wall Street, 28th Floor
New York, NY 10005
USA

mail-usa@austinmacauley.com
+1 (646) 5125767

The following are those who assisted and mentored me throughout my career. The late Sgt. Luis Albuerne, who took an interest in mentoring me, Maj. John Burhmaster, Maj. Mario Garcia, State Attorneys Gary Winston, Michael Van Zampt, Gail Levine, Maggie Gerson, Alejandra Lopez, and the late David Waksman. The doctors of the Miami-Dade Medical Examiner's Office, Valerie J. Rao, M.D., and the late Bruce A. Hyma, M.D. and Joseph H. Davis, M.D. A special acknowledgment to the doctors and staff of The City of New York Office of Chief Medical Examiner. I especially want to thank Emma O. Lew, M.D. and Nicole Scott Dixon, J.D., who always found time to answer all of my questions and took their time to review my work.

Chapter 1
Mental Preparation

When discussing the 'mental preparation' of a violent crime's investigator, what are the questions that an investigator must ask? One can say that mental preparation commences when the investigator receives the first call of a death investigation or violent incident. That is a valid and logical assumption, but beyond the simplicity of that, where do we begin the process of 'mental preparation?' These are questions that an investigator, regardless of experience, must find a way to answer before his or her day starts. There are aspects of working death or violent crime investigations that will tax an investigators' mental, physical, and spiritual health. With this in mind, let us take a few moments to journey through an investigator's 'mental preparation.'

As a homicide investigator, one has to be prepared for a multitude of issues that arise at any death scene. It is very important to have the right frame of mind when taking on the responsibility as the lead investigator. How can one be mentally ready prior to arriving on a death scene? This question must be answered well before any investigation begins.

Each death or violent crime investigation takes on different dynamics throughout the course of the investigation.

From a natural death, which is one of the easiest cases to investigate, to the more complex investigation, such as a homicide, that could potentially have multiple victims and scenes.

An investigator is always thinking of how to work an investigation in order to achieve a positive result. But when the investigator is out with family and friends or trying to enjoy his or her time off (which is rare), they must constantly have a prepared game plan, a ritual of sorts that brings them into focus for the task at hand. One perceives that when they watch a crime drama on the television or in the cinema, that what the investigator is doing can be accomplished by anyone, which is not the case. Unfortunately, the movie industry would have you think so.

Attaining the status of a violent crime or death investigator, a.k.a. homicide detective, takes many years of training and learning prepares one for the challenges that each case brings. Wearing a badge with the word 'investigator' really does not mean anything if the one wearing it does not know what they are doing. Investigators lie awake countless nights, dreading the call that a death has occurred. Well, this is what death investigators must be prepared to confront. Death investigations must be a passion, not just a title. Investigators love their profession, even knowing what they are exposed to can create psychological barriers with family, friends, and co-workers. It is for these reasons that very few investigators make a career of working in a violent crime's unit. The nature of the work takes a toll on everyone.

However, for those investigators who are able to overcome the toils of a career in violent crimes, they become the standard by which other investigators, regular officers, and individuals from outside agencies gauge success. The hard work and dedication of an investigator will always shine, even if they do not solve every case.

So, how does an investigator prepare to work a death investigation? Let us start by identifying the various types of death cases that an investigator will be dealing with. Death investigators work such cases as *natural deaths, unclassified deaths, undetermined deaths, accidental deaths, suicides,* and *homicides.* Each investigator, knowing that they can be called to work at any time, must approach each incident in a methodical manner. The investigator must know that the responsibility they assumed, as a professional investigator, is one of genuine caring for the victim or victims of each case. The investigator must also have profound empathy for the relatives of the victim(s). They are the ones that have to be a part of an unpleasant journey with the lead investigator, from the inception of the investigation until it reaches the trial phase. The investigator needs to understand that Next of Kin (N.O.K.) have an expectation that not only will the investigator conduct a complete and thorough investigation, but they will be continuously informed of how the investigation is progressing. Another key point that cannot be overlooked, does the next of kin have crucial information that can assist in the investigation?

The investigator who has properly prepared for each investigation starts by knowing the city in which they work. Each investigator must know and understand the makeup and dynamics of the citizens that live where they work. Who are the citizens? Are they predominantly African American, White, Latino, Asian, Haitian, Jewish, Muslim, other ethnicities, or a rich vibrant mixture of all? This information is crucial to the way that the investigator approaches each case. Investigators must be able to comfortably interact with all people. Another factor that comes into play, the socio-economic status of the city where they work (affluent, middle-class, or low income). This should not play an important role in the investigator's approach because investigators must be totally objective. There is something to be said, about the city, where the investigator conducts his/her investigation. Why? If an investigator does not possess the tools to interact with a variety of people, then he/she is laying the foundation for failure. An investigator must be able to conduct a professional, unbiased investigation no matter whom he/she meets. The investigation must take precedence over all else, not who is involved, or who is the family and friends. If an investigator cannot have a proper and civil conversation with members of the community, how does one think the investigation is going to evolve? Surely, it would be safe to guess that the investigation will not go well. Interaction with peoples of all backgrounds is crucial and the cornerstone of each investigation. The moment that an investigator cannot deal with the simplicity of a civil, verbal exchange during the inception of an investigation, all is lost. The investigator must remember that social or ethnic class has no part on how an investigation is to be conducted.

Truly, it is important that an investigator acquires a well-rounded understanding of the citizens of the city where an investigation is being conducted.

Another important factor that should be discussed is the type of area where the investigation is taking place, from the opulence of marble to the tattered slums of boarding and section eight housing. If an investigator is not prepared to understand the differences, then the investigation will suffer. How wonderful it would be if every investigation were conducted in an environment that was fully air-conditioned, sterile, and in museum-like conditions. Unfortunately, in the real world, such conditions are far and few in between. An investigator's approach changes based on the location where an investigation will be taking place, such as an apartment complex, townhome community, or warehouse districts. All these locations pose a different approach than a regular residential area. Other factors that come into play are areas where civilian traffic is high, such as shopping centers, grocery stores, schools, locations of worship, and a multitude of other locations. It is important for the investigators to have a good idea and knowledge of these areas because they can better prepare the initial approach of the investigation. Also, does the city where an investigation is going to take place surrounded by water (beaches/lakes) or waterways such as rivers or canals. An investigator must consider these additional factors.

The factors previously listed are crucial to an investigator. Based on those factors, the investigator must understand the location of where the crime took place. What is the make-up of the citizens in said area and what special needs will be required? It is important for an investigator to continuously run mental scenarios in order to be better prepared to formulate a plan of action prior to arriving at any location within his/her city of operation. Remembering that no two investigations are alike, an investigator must have a mental checklist that he/she can run off in order to bring out the proper equipment or resources needed to aid with an investigation.

I suggest that an investigator routinely take an area in his/her city and initiate a mental scenario of a multitude of incidents. As the investigator runs these mental exercises, he/she should be going through a checklist of things that could be needed in order to commence the investigation. The importance of this exercise is so that the investigator maintains a fluid list in his/her mind of significant resources needed, as well as items. By having a continuous mental course, the investigator most likely will not have surprises pop-up when he/she responds to a real incident. Starting by ensuring that the crime scene has been properly secured. Based on the size of the crime scene, are additional officers or investigators needed to assist with the investigation. Where will the staging area be set for police, media, fire rescue, medical examiner, crime scene and state attorney? Will a Mobile Command Vehicle (M.C.V.) be needed? These are a few essential questions that the investigator must be ready to answer.

This section has discussed a few mental aspects of the 'mental preparation.' However, is that all that an investigator needs to be ready? I submit to the would-be investigator that there is much more.

In addition to being mentally prepared, the investigator must be physically ready to take on the grueling challenge of either a short-term investigation or a prolonged investigation. Let me be clear, "There truly is *no short-term* investigation." All investigations, no matter how simple, takes many hours to complete. In order for the investigator to maintain a continuous upbeat tempo, his/her physical stamina must be at an optimal level. Why would I say that? The reason is quite simple. During a tour of duty, an investigator is asked to investigate a simple natural death, but during the course of the investigation, the next of kin was not located. Therefore, what would have been several hours of investigating a simple case turns into 10-14 hours of investigation in order to identify family that can better describe any medical history that the victim might have. Another reason, an investigator has been working his/her regular shift (usually 10 hours) and while on the way home from a long day, he/she is asked to return to work because of another type of death investigation. During the course of this investigation, Crime-Scene Investigation (C.S.I.), Medical Examiner (M.E.), and the on-call Assistant State Attorney (A.S.A.) must be summoned to the location of the incident. This process takes hours and before the investigator realizes, he/she has worked 20-24 hours straight, went home to clean up and returned to work. At the end, the investigator has worked over 30 hours continuously without rest. If the investigator were not physically ready, he/she would be unable to complete the investigative task. Granted, it is not every day that an investigator works 20-30 hours straight, but when one tallies an investigator's regular shift, time spent in court or regular follow-ups on other cases, a regular week can turn from 40 hours to 60 hours. Considering this, if an investigator maintains a workout regimen and good sleeping habits, then the physical strain becomes more manageable. Understanding that each investigator has a framed work schedule, a workout schedule, if possible, should be a part of the investigator's regular routine. Such workouts are great for reenergizing.

When discussing the spiritual approach or well-being of the investigator, the suggestion is not one of religion, although religion can play a part for some. The spiritual wellbeing for an investigator is one of internal peace. How to properly cope with what he/she is about to see and touch. Putting cases in perspective, the average investigator will investigate at least two-three types of death cases per week, multiplied by 52 weeks in a year, and it is conceivable that an investigator will probe over 100 death cases. These numbers can fluctuate depending on the area in which an investigator works. The numbers could be greater and, in some cases, fewer. Nonetheless, the amount of death scenes that an investigator explores during the course of his/her career could conceivably cause some investigators to be diagnosed with Post Traumatic Stress Disorder (P.T.S.D.). If one puts this in perspective, there is truly no difference with the amount of carnage seen by an investigator or a soldier in combat. The circumstances are different, but the gore and carnage remains the same. Those images can haunt an investigator in one way or another, and the reason why it is so important for an investigator to be emotionally grounded.

There was a time when investigators would gather at their nearest watering hole (bar) in order to take the edge off a very difficult shift. Well, this presents another problem. After a few drinks, the investigator needs to drive home, not a good idea. Once home, the investigator becomes distant from those that are closest to them. Sometimes, verbal and mental abuse occurs.

Unfortunately, this is a defensive mechanism in order to shun others out of the difficult and cruel aspects of cases that are being investigated. There is no calming conversation that an investigator can have with individuals, especially, if those persons have no idea of what the investigator is referring to.

So, during these times, who does the investigator turn to? A simple suggestion is to find a hobby, workout, read, simply spend quality time with love ones, and yes, for some investigators, religion gives them a sense of peace. There is no real answer to what I refer to as the spiritual wellbeing. Every investigator must find their inner place where he/she can become grounded, at peace, and understand the craft that has been chosen is a calling that not many can do well.

Early in this section, you read that an investigator could be out enjoying much needed time with family and friends when they receive a call to respond to a death scene. The importance of the investigator's relationship with his family plays a vital role on how an investigator will focus. It is true that while the investigator has the responsibility to answer the call of duty and respond to the scene, the family does not. The investigator needs to have a solid partnership with his/her family if they want to succeed. The investigator needs to have a serious conversation with their family prior to embarking on the process of joining a homicide unit and for that matter, any investigative unit. This conversation is important because they need to understand the enormous responsibility of an investigator. The investigator must include his/her family in this undertaking, because, families are impacted in a way that is not readily understandable. Even after these conversations take place and everyone is onboard with the decision that an investigator has taken, issues still arise. How difficult will it be for an investigator to tell his/her child that they cannot attend a school function or special event? What happens when the investigator is attending a birthday party and abruptly needs to leave? Most of all, what happens when the investigator is about to attend an anniversary dinner and the dreaded call is received? These critical questions need to be answered well before one embarks on becoming an investigator. The investigator's family is the most important component in the investigator's mental make-up. If there are any issues or concerns at home because of the responsibilities that come during the course of any investigation, then the investigation will not receive the attention needed, and the investigator would not have fulfilled his responsibility.

'Mental preparation' takes on a life of its own, it takes many years of behavioral modification, and discipline for an investigator to reach the level of comfort it takes to assume the responsibility of a 'homicide investigator' or any other major crime's investigator. One must be well grounded to accept what one is about to receive. Investigators must have the passion to perform their task, knowing full well that nothing is owed to them. Therefore, they must be mentally prepared for the challenge.

Chapter 2
Crime Scene
(Initial Response)

Upon receiving the call that a violent crime has taken place, it is important for the investigator to start documenting every bit of information that is received. One of the tools that is crucial is what I like to refer to as 'the Bible' (a notebook for documenting events and times). Therefore, as an investigator responding to a crime scene, their responsibility is to ensure patrol units who are on the scene have properly secured the crime scene. As an investigator, you must start mentally preparing for what you might encounter upon arrival. During the mental preparation phase, the investigator can begin to develop a plan of action of how the investigation will start. For this reason, it is crucial that the investigator have a good working relationship with the crime--scene technician during the course of the investigation. In working the crime scene, they need to be in constant communication and understand how and why the scene investigation is progressing in a specific manner. *One important aspect to understand as an investigator; you are at a crime scene to investigate the crime and not to process the crime scene, that is left to those with the expertise in that field. However, an investigator must have a working knowledge of crime-scene processing if they are to effectively collaborate with the lead crime-scene technician.

However, before we go any further, let us understand that prior to police or fire rescue arriving on a crime scene, someone was in the crime scene and felt that a crime had taken place. Once the notion was felt, then 911 was called. Initial contamination of the crime scene occurred at precisely the moment a person or persons, not related to the incident, were present. Therefore, as an investigator, you have to start thinking along the lines of who initially was in the scene. However, this question needs to be answered at some point during the course of the investigation.

As patrol officers arrive on a scene, they will determine if a crime has taken place. They need to ensure that there is no imminent danger prior to allowing fire rescue to attend to the injured victim or before they proceed to secure the crime scene. This is when the on-scene officer(s) will notify the investigator responding to the scene. After briefly explaining to the investigator what has taken place, the investigator will advise the officer to notify crime-scene personnel (Crime-Scene Investigations). In the interim, it is the responsibility of the first units on the scene to secure the crime scene in order to preserve the scene's integrity. A good rule to follow when securing a scene is to make it as big as possible. It is easier for the scene to be reduced once the lead investigator determines what is acceptable, rather than trying to extend a crime scene. Keep in mind that a crime scene can be adversely contaminated if it is not contained properly, that means; if a crime scene is kept small, then any possible evidence outside the initial area can theoretically be lost or contaminated. In addition, if people are allowed to enter or exit a crime scene, this too can be a problem for the integrity of a crime scene. This includes officers or command-staff personnel that just want to see what is going on.

Let there be no doubt, crime scenes are complex. It does not matter how small or large they might be. Crime scenes range from a small space, such as a bathroom, to as large as a field. These enormous differences in scale can pose a problem and create difficulties when securing and processing such a scene. The gravity of a poorly secured crime scene can cause an investigation to fail. Remember that this is a basic introduction to crime-scene investigations for the aspiring investigator. Therefore, it is crucial that an investigator receive as much training as possible in the area of crime-scene investigations. An investigator must be on the same page as a crime-scene technician, this allows for a free flow of ideas and a check and balance process.

Upon arriving at a crime scene, it is the responsibility of the lead investigator to select an area away from the crime scene in order to meet with the investigative team, which would include crime-scene investigators. This isolated location is selected in order to gather initial information, exchange ideas, and assign tasks to those charged with the investigation. This location is where the lead investigator meets with the primary officer. The primary officer will brief the investigating team as to what had been learned prior to the teams' arrival. Once the team receives the initial briefing, the lead investigator, his team, and the lead crime-scene technician will do a cursory walkthrough of the crime scene. This is done in order to get an overview of the scene's dynamics. Once the walkthrough is completed, the lead investigator or a designee will brief the agency's command staff.

The importance of the crime scene cannot be emphasized enough and it is important to maintain the security of any crime scene until the lead investigator is comfortable in allowing it to be released (opened up).

Moving forward, we will be discussing the approach to the crime scene, its importance and the value placed on why certain methods are used to process a scene. We have established that the most important thing is to preserve the integrity of a crime scene. This means that people, regardless if they are officers or civilians, must be kept from entering or exiting a crime scene, ensuring that crime scene tape has been placed along the furthest part of a crime scene for security purposes. In addition, there are instances when a crime scene can have an inner and outer perimeter as well as an area for media and command staff to gather. During the initial stages of an investigation, there could come a time where additional crime scenes are found related to the initial incident. These can be found during the initial canvassing stage.

The lead investigators' responsibility at the crime scene is to ensure that no hazards are in the crime scene, if additional scenes have been located and their priority. Work force is always an issue at a crime scene, especially if there are multiple scenes or the initial scene is large. Once the lead investigator begins the second walkthrough of the scene with the lead crime scene technician, they will evaluate what is of importance, and what is needed to begin the process. It is important to remember that equipment, manpower, and special services must have special considerations in order to properly process a crime scene. These considerations are dependent upon the type of crime scene (crime), location(s), types of evidence, hazards, weather conditions, or if the incident has attracted a large or unruly type of civilian spectators. Another important factor is whether a search warrant will be needed (we will discuss search warrant considerations later).

Crucial information needed is whether items were collected or moved by any officer or rescue personnel prior to the investigator's arrival on the scene. The investigator must document where the items were upon their arrival. They should then make contact with any personnel that moved items and attempt to get the exact location where said item(s) were prior to removal. Personnel that move items should be mandated to write a detailed supplemental report and be as accurate as possible, to include position of items and where the items were located. The investigator must find out if, by moving the item(s), it altered the appearance or structure of said item(s).

The documentation of a crime scene is of paramount importance in order to accurately immortalize how the investigator viewed it on the date of the incident in question. An investigator must take copious notes upon their arrival, the scene (to include a diagram – not to scale), who has been contacted, and what is observed. Once on the scene and once the initial notes have been taken, the investigator(s) need to find a location, not far from the scene, to gather their thoughts and confer with additional team members as they arrive. This area can be inside the Mobile Command Vehicle (M.C.V.), on the trunk of the lead investigator(s) vehicle, or any location away from the crowd of officers or command-staff personnel that want to be given information prior to facts being gathered. Unfortunately, command staff is often more of a hindrance than help on the scene of a major crime because they feel they need to be given information, even if that information must be updated multiple times over. It is amazing how personnel at the command-staff level, who have never had the responsibility of being a lead investigator of a major crime investigation, feel entitled to information before it is vetted.

For this reason, it is crucial that investigator(s) document who is in the scene and what their purpose was. If, for reasons beyond the control of the lead investigator, personnel walk in a crime scene, those individuals must be documented in the initial report. They must be mandated to write a detailed supplement as to why they entered the crime scene without authorization from the investigative team.

After the investigative team concludes their initial briefing, the lead investigator or team supervisor will assign a co-lead. Once assignments have been given, the initial walk-through of the crime scene is done. During this walk-through, notes are taken by each team member in order to memorialize what they have observed. Remember, only the lead investigator and his team are allowed to enter the crime scene at this point. Upon conclusion of the first walk-through, the team will again gather and determine what types of equipment might be needed. They will discuss observations made and who will interview potential witnesses or living victim(s). It is important to understand that if an investigator is not familiar with the particulars of a scene, then they will not be able to ask questions or follow-up questions to those witnesses or living victim(s) being interviewed. As a reminder, the initial walk-through is to gather scene information and document what is observed. One limits the amount of personnel into a crime scene to prevent any loss of evidence or the introduction of evidence that has no relevance to the case, such as personnel smoking inside a scene, discarding cigarettes, leaving candy wrappers, or food. One would be surprised to learn how many cases are contaminated with items that are not part of the incident because of negligence of the first officers on scene or a careless investigator.

A good example of contaminating a crime scene is an officer, investigator, or rescue personnel stepping into a pool of blood and tracking the floor, leaving shoe impressions. Another example is an officer or anyone else that smokes and drops the cigarette in the scene. One can see the problem with this scenario since everything must be documented and is discoverable (turning everything over to the defense prior to trial, this is called discovery). Unfortunately, if the investigator is unable to rule out what is or is not a part of the crime, the defense attorney can create reasonable doubt and the case can be lost during court proceedings.

This is the reason an investigative team leader needs to determine from which point to enter a crime scene and where to exit the scene to cause the least amount of disturbance within the crime scene. Most likely, unless the scene is an outdoor scene, an investigator can determine from where the offender entered and exited the crime scene. Emphasis at this point should be placed on locating physical evidence of value that must be documented and collected for further analysis.

Once the initial walk-through of the crime scene has been completed by the investigative team, they should regroup and conduct a briefing of what they learned, observed, and which investigator will be given specific assignments. These assignments can be, staying on the scene until it has been completely processed by the crime-scene investigations unit, conducting an area canvass for additional evidence, interviewing possible witness(s), or going to the hospital to meet with trauma-team personnel.

During the course of the initial investigation, if the lead investigator is able to obtain additional information that is crucial to the scene investigation, then he/she must advise the lead crime-scene technician. This information can determine how the technician will proceed with the processing and how much weight is placed on the information learned. It is important to understand that during the processing of the scene, information obtained must immediately be passed on to the lead investigator or crime-scene technician. The continuous flow of information makes for a better partnership between the investigative team and the processing team. This information is valuable in giving credence to any information learned during the investigation; it can be used to refute what is said by witness(s) or subject(s) when they are interviewed.

The outcome of any investigation can be directly attributed to the information gathered and documented on a crime scene. It is the responsibility of the lead investigator to share any information with those involved with the investigation in order to bring about a positive result. The importance of sharing information during the initial stage of an investigation, especially during the processing of the crime scene, can determine the result of the case. Remember that once a crime scene is released and evidence has not been collected, that evidence is lost. An investigator cannot go back and introduce evidence into a crime scene. This is a 'No-No.'

Once the lead investigator meets with the lead crime-scene technician and they have discussed all that has been done on the crime scene, then and only then can the crime scene be released. The final determination of releasing a crime scene is the responsibility of the lead investigator. They have the authority to hold a scene for as long as they determine that evidence can be obtained.

Section 2

It is important and crucial for the crime scene to be documented properly and evidence identified. As previously discussed, it is important to communicate with the lead crime-scene technician prior to releasing a crime scene, regardless of the type of crime. For this reason, the lead investigator must canvass the crime scene as many times as they feel necessary, and as noted earlier, the lead investigator can hold a crime scene for as long as it is needed. So, when we speak about canvassing a crime scene or areas adjacent to the crime scene, what do we mean? Why is it important? The lead investigator and his team have a responsibility to ensure that every possible piece of evidence is located, documented, and collected. In order for this to occur, the investigators must have a keen sense of observation and not overlook items or dismiss items as non-valuable. Anything and everything should be considered evidence, until it is determined that it is not.

Identifying evidence is crucial, the investigative team and lead crime-scene technician must examine the information that they have obtained by the officers that initially responded to the crime scene. During the initial team briefing, this information must be analyzed. Assignments on how to proceed with the canvass will be given to the investigators. A lead investigator has the responsibility to inform the lead crime-scene technician of how the initial canvass will be conducted. Mental preparation plays a big role during this phase of the investigation. If an investigator has a clear picture of the location where the crime took place, then they can better assess how and where to look for possible clues that will assist in the investigation.

Investigators must depend on the power of observation if they are going to be successful. A crime scene must be canvassed in a methodical manner. The system or method used to canvass can vary but it must be done in such a manner that every possible section is searched. Even with these practices, there will be times when evidence can be missed, but we can discuss that later. Being consistent is crucial when conducting an area canvass. Consistency is paramount to ensure uniformity in the way that an area canvass is conducted. This will be helpful when providing testimony, either at a deposition or during trial.

Whether you are the first officer on the crime scene or a seasoned investigator, the manner in which you interpret what you see in a crime scene will assist you in possibly solving crimes. It is always about the little things and the investigator's ability to understand what they are looking at that can affect the outcome of the investigation. The way in which an investigator approaches a crime scene is paramount and the key that gets the investigation going.

As a lead investigator or a member of the team working a violent crime, it is important to document any and all information received. Based on the information, the investigator can begin to formulate a plan of how to proceed with the area canvass and how to give out assignments to the other investigator's assisting, and in some cases, uniform patrol can be utilized. Upon receiving the initial information regarding the crime scene, type of crime, and having done the initial walk-through of the crime scene, most of your key questions should be noted and answered.

The lead investigator must know the area that is to be searched. Once the area of concern is identified, then a search can commence. The lead investigator's responsibility is to assign specific areas to his team. This method has a two-fold reason. The first being that one or two investigators can take a section of the location to be searched and it can be done methodically and faster. The second reason allows for investigators to cover a smaller area and they are able to possibly locate and document where evidence, such as strike marks, fingerprints, footprints, serological, or any other type of physical evidence is located. Remember that evidence can be located on walls, ceilings, floors, and clothing on people, or anywhere inside the crime scene. Once evidence has been identified, the lead crime-scene technician is able to proceed with the processing and collecting of evidence. It is always good practice to have the lead crime-scene technician or other technicians assigned to the incident, document, process, and collect the evidence. This allows chain of custody to be consistent. Another reason chain of custody is important: once the case goes to trial, it should be the responsibility of the lead crime-scene technician to introduce the evidence that was collected. It just makes it easier.

Always remember that when a crime scene is being canvassed or searched, there is the possibility that valuable evidence can be lost. This occurs by stepping on evidence, driving on evidence, or simply and unknowingly touching and moving evidence. Keep in mind, once evidence has been disturbed, altered, or touched, it has been *contaminated.* Contaminating any part of a crime scene is a critical error that cannot be fixed. This is why, once a crime scene is secured, NO ONE is allowed to enter the area without the permission of the lead investigator regardless of what position/rank one has.

As a lead investigator or a member of the investigative team, YOU ARE NOT A CRIME-SCENE TECHNICIAN; therefore, it is important that any processing of the crime scene be left to those that are qualified to do so. This is not to say that when there is no crime-scene technician available or the crime scene is small, that an investigator or patrol officer, especially if the crime is not major in scope; such as a simple burglary or auto theft, can start a basic procedure of processing (photographs and dust for prints).

During the initial stages of any investigation, information gathered from witnesses or living victims is paramount. That information, when pieced together with other bits of data gathered, can be extremely helpful in locating areas where evidence can best be located and documented. As the investigators gather information, once witnesses and living victims have been interviewed, additional information can be obtained from first responders that arrived on the scene to render assistance. That means, fire-rescue personnel, police officers, or public-works employees can be interviewed to obtain important information regarding the crime scene.

It is during the interview phase of the investigation and before investigators enter the crime scene with the lead crime-scene technician, that all information is documented (immortalized) and can be explained by the investigator or those that were interviewed. Remember, during depositions and trial, questions will be asked and they need to be answered. Everything that is observed by the investigators is crucial. Why? Because as a person who does not live, visit, or directly knows the location in question, the observation and documentation can tell the story. Everything in the crime scene should be foreign to the investigators as well as the crime-scene technician.

The lead investigator must rely on their life experience to better understand what does and does not belong at a crime scene, for instance, it is safe to say that a butcher knife belongs in a kitchen and not a bathroom. Tools belong inside a toolbox, in a garage, or storage shed, as opposed to under a window that has been pried open or shattered. Furniture is set in a certain manner inside a home or business. Therefore, when the lead investigator observes furniture strewn about, questions should start to formulate in the investigators' mind as to what might have taken place. An investigator must use their power of observation and common sense if they are to achieve a good sense of how a crime scene might have looked prior to the critical event-taking place.

The lead investigator needs to approach the crime scene as a large puzzle, what belongs where and why it was moved or disturbed. How can the puzzle be put together in order to capture the original state of the crime scene prior to the crime taken place? The manner in which an investigator observes the crime scene will always dictate the approach of how to proceed with the search of the scene.

It is always important to understand the type of crime that is being investigated and where it took place. This will determine the approach for documenting and collecting evidence. An investigator needs to know the types of evidence that can be found on a scene, such as fingerprints, trace evidence, transfer evidence (this can be paint from one vehicle to another), casings, projectiles, strike marks, blood, or any other type of D.N.A. evidence. Remember that most crime-scene technicians carry special equipment in their crime-scene vans and use several methods to extract evidence. This can be from a metal detector to superglue.

In my thirty-five years of experience working major crimes, I have used several methods to properly and thoroughly search a crime scene. I have also spoken to a multitude of investigators and crime-scene technicians that employ the same procedure. The following techniques are some of the ones that are used.

Spiral Search: this search starts at a central point and as one walks around and out from the point of origin, they end up at a point that has covered the desired area. I have not used this technique often, but it is effective, especially when people trampling around prior to the search have not disturbed the area being search.

Zone Search: this type of search requires the search area to be divided into zones two, four, six, etc. Each quadrant is then measured into 4x4 feet, 6x6 feet, or 2x2 feet, and once this is done, the investigator searches each zone until they are satisfied before they move on. I have used this technique in an open field and it has been used by divers when searching the sea floor for discarded evidence (guns, knives, and clothing).

Strip Search: this technique is performed by going in one direction and does not cover the same area twice. This might be a good technique for a flat, open surface such as a road or concrete patio, where one can observe everything in sight. Best used during daylight hours or when the crime scene is highly illuminated.

Grid Search: this type of search is the most common and effective. One conducts this search by walking slowly in a straight path from point A to point B, once you have reached point B, you turn and return toward point A. The next phase is to conduct the same pattern but perpendicular to the first pattern. These patterns are repeated multiple times until you have covered the desired area. This is one of my favorite techniques. The secret to this technique is to walk slowly, keep a tight line when walking, and document everything that is out of place. One can repeat this technique but like anything else, once you walk over an area, it is now disturbed. This technique is much like the Strip Search, but covers more area within the same space.

Patience is a large component of a good search. The lead investigator has to ensure that those that are assigned a particular area do not rush. It does not matter so long as the crime scene is secured. Just keep in mind, once the crime scene has been released, ALL is lost and cannot be recreated (this means that the likelihood of contamination increases). Investigators must always be vigilant when conducting a search inside a crime scene. They should question everything that they observe and remember to question anyone that was part of the initial response. Nothing in a crime scene should be taken for granted or dismissed without properly vetting. The investigator must have a working knowledge of what a crime-scene technician needs to perform their duties while on a crime scene. As stated earlier, a major crime investigator is not crime-scene trained, by working closely with the crime-scene unit, there comes a time when this working relationship allows for a very good understanding of what can and cannot be done on a crime scene. Also, the types of tools and equipment needed to perform the task at hand, such as camera, flashlight, fingerprint kit, metal detector, numbered cones/markers, multiple types of hand tools, rakes, various types of shovels, knife, strings, rope, rods, and industrial-type light fixtures (for scenes with minimal or no lighting).

Section 3

As an investigator, the crime scene has to be properly documented. Everything that is observed inside a crime scene must be immortalized in some way or another. The investigators' responsibilities are to ensure that what they observe is noted in the 'Bible' (daily notepad) so that it can be transposed later to the final supplemental report. Unlike crime-scene technicians, investigators normally do not photograph or take measurements of a crime scene, but what they can do, is make rough sketches (not to scale) in order for them to refresh their memory as the investigation progresses. Crime-scene technicians utilize methods such as photography, measuring tools, and videotaping. These methods are crucial to an investigation and to the lead investigator.

Once the lead investigator commences the on-scene documentation, they must take into account that what they write must be discussed with the lead crime-scene technician. In cases such as homicide investigations, it is important that only one person on the investigative team write locations of where items were located, to include the victim. Then, the investigator can draw a rough sketch. This might seem as excessive, but when the investigative team briefs with the lead crime-scene technician, it is crucial to have all notes compared in order to ensure that the crime scene has been thoroughly processed. During the many briefings that will be conducted prior to the releasing of the crime scene, investigators can analyze what they have learned. If everything appears to be in order, then the investigation will proceed, if something does not seem right, then it is time to pause, evaluate, and discuss the concerns before continuing.

Once the investigator starts to document the crime scene, they must include everything that they see. It has always been my practice to begin from the exterior and work my way inside or to where the victims' final resting point is. Consider that there might be multiple victims, deceased or alive, when documenting. So, once on the scene, the investigator has a responsibility to begin from outside the crime scene and work their way in. Now, what do I mean by that? On the exterior part of the scene, the investigator documents (draws and writes) the street, intersections, swales, sidewalks, homes or buildings, and utility poles (with their numbers). Keep in mind that as the scene scribe (sketch does not need to be done by the lead investigator, but his designee), they are not artistic, all that is needed is a good sketch to use as a guide. The official sketch will be produced by the lead crime-scene technician. Attempt to keep lines straight and curves as close as possible. Sidewalks and swales are important, especially if casings and strike marks are observed. When sketching the exterior of houses, include the walkway and driveway if applicable. DO NOT add anything that does not belong. Make sure that vehicles are added too, include the numbers on the license plate.

The lead investigator's rough sketch is important because it allows the team to refresh what they observed during the initial canvass. All items that are documented in the investigator's rough sketch do not always make it to the final official sketch of the lead crime-scene technician. During the phase of documenting the rough sketch, items such as strike marks (location where bullet(s) impact), blood patterns (droplets, spatter, cast-off), casings, bullets, fragments, weapons, vehicles, or any item that may be a part of the crime, must be documented as to their location in relationship to the primary scene. As stated before, the crime scene can be very large in scale, but the primary scene might be inside the original area that was cordoned off. So, anything that might be of evidentiary value must be documented.

The final product will be created by the lead crime-scene technician, but it is important for the lead investigator to have an idea of what the final sketch will look like. Only items of significant importance should be included in the final sketch, this avoids clutter and confusion. In reviewing the final sketch, it should be prepared in such a manner that what is seen can be easy to translate to persons that were never at the crime scene. A layperson, upon seeing the sketch, should be able to understand what the lead investigator observed. Included in sketches are points of entry and exit, such as doors and windows (this should be done for all crime scenes that are processed). Furniture and its position inside the crime scene or outside, that is crucial to the investigation, must be included in the final sketch. Items that have no relevance to the crime scene should not be included in the final sketch.

Documentation of crimes scenes are important and vital to properly investigating any crime. Though we have discussed rough sketches and final sketches, do not feel that you will become a crime-scene technician, which is another profession within law enforcement. The main reason for discussing sketches and documentation is to ensure that as an investigator, you are well versed in what everyone is doing while on a crime scene and what specific responsibilities each person has. As the lead investigator of any incident, when you turn in your final product (case file) to the prosecuting attorney, everything within that case file should be precise, accurate, and truthful. Your reputation counts on it!

Section 4

Recognizing that as an investigator, you are not a crime-scene technician, you should have a working knowledge or some expertise as to what evidence is of value or not. During the observation phase of your crime-scene search, there will come a time when you observe possible evidence such as fingerprints. These fingerprints could be from people that legitimately belong at the scene (house, apartment, business, etc.) or from possible subjects that have no business inside the location. Consider that fingerprints can also be located in any outdoor crime scene, this can include vehicles, trailers, windows, or any discarded items that were observed during the initial search/canvass. Weather conditions are important when dealing with outdoor scenes. The investigator must keep in mind that inconveniences such as rain, early morning dew, and even dust, will delay the ability to lift latent prints.

Since we have touched on fingerprints, what does the investigator need to know? Fingerprints have been around for centuries, and it takes a true professional to extract (lift) good prints. Just because some powder is spread on a crime scene, that does not mean that good fingerprints will be extracted. A good crime-scene technician and to some degree, a seasoned investigator, can determine if fingerprints located in a crime scene are of evidentiary value. The prints extracted by the crime-scene technician must be taken to the examination room in order to have a latent I.D. examiner review and determine if the prints, that were lifted, were of value or not.

In consultation with a multitude of crime-scene supervisors and years of reviewing documents regarding fingerprints, let us concede the following; there are three types of fingerprint groups and no two people have the same fingerprints. The three groups are *whorls, arches,* and *loops.* In discussing these groups, there are various types such as; plain arches, tented arches, ulnar loops, radial loops, plain whorls, double-loop whorls, central pocket-loop whorls, and accidental whorls. Now, I am not an expert crime-scene technician and this is not a crime-scene instructional, but it is extremely important for an investigator to be able to speak the same language with the crime-scene technician. A true investigator, who wants to be considered very good at their craft, must take time to read about how crime scenes are processed and what can and cannot be done. As an investigator, one must spend many hours asking questions and watching how crime-scene technicians work. The investigator must not feel intimidated because of the lack of knowledge in this field, but should make it a point to always have questions ready to be asked.

In all of my years as a homicide investigator, I have had the opportunity to work with many excellent crime-scene technicians. During our many briefings and cases that we have worked together, I learned that three types of fingerprints could be found in a crime scene. These fingerprints are *visible prints, impression prints*, and *latent prints.* The importance of knowing about these prints is to understand what prints can be found within a crime scene. The investigator should be able to communicate with the crime-scene technician and understand what is being discussed. Therefore, the following definitions will help in better understanding each type of print.

Visible Print: The impression of a fingerprint that can normally be located in fluids such as blood, grease, paint, or any other type where fingerprints are readily visible. This type of fingerprint normally is photographed, and then collected with the item that it is on.

Impression Print: This type of fingerprint is located in wax or clay, and will become a three-dimensional impression. This type of fingerprint normally is photographed, and then collected with the item that it is on.

Latent Print: This type of fingerprint is not readily visible to the naked eye. These prints are the most common and are enhanced by applying powder, chemicals, or lighting techniques. Like all fingerprints, once they are developed, then they are photographed and lifted with fingerprint tape. The tape is then adhered to a plain-white index card.

Investigators need to know that these are not the only ways to recover fingerprints; there are many other methods, especially when dealing with porous or nonporous surfaces. This is where the relationship between the lead investigator and the crime-scene technician becomes so important. During the briefings at the crime scene, this is where strategies must be discussed if evidence is to be obtained. This is the time when the use of Ninhydrin, laser, or ultraviolet lighting can be discussed (for porous surfaces) or cyanoacrylate fuming/dye, vacuum metal deposition (V.M.D.), laser or alternate light source (for nonporous surfaces). These are but a few techniques that can be discussed at a crime scene. Keep in mind that there are many different methods to extract fingerprints and if an investigator truly wants to know all, then they should request to attend a crime-scene technician course. *These are guidelines for investigators to have a better understanding, not designed to make them crime-scene technicians.

Section 5

The lead investigator must take into account all aspects of a crime-scene investigation and what items are of value and which ones are not. During the processing of a crime scene, investigators must communicate with the lead crime-scene technician in order to confirm what items of evidence will be processed and collected. As the crime-scene technician prepares to collect evidence, they will advise the lead investigator or an investigative team designee to ensure that they are aware of the evidence being collected. Consider that *chain of custody* is important, this allows for evidence to be processed and collected by one person and limits any arguments by the defense attorney of contamination or manipulation of the evidence.

During the processing stages at a crime scene, investigators will discuss procedures such as collection and packaging of evidence with the lead crime-scene technician. These are two different tasks. Keep in mind that as a crime scene is being processed, a lead investigator needs to ensure that all the evidence is transported to the property section or evidence room for proper storage. This must be done in a methodical and thoughtful manner to ensure for the integrity of the investigation and so that there can be no doubt, as to how the evidence was processed, collected, packaged, and stored. Reverting to my many years working closely with crime-scene technicians, I have been able to observe how they package evidence. Not all evidence is packaged in the same manner.

Evidence that is collected must be packaged in such a way that it can be stored and preserved for future analysis without fear that it may deteriorate before it can be introduced during court proceedings. As a lead investigator, always remember that the responsibility of the case ultimately falls on you. Investigators do not have the luxury of shifting the responsibility once they are on the witness stand during a trial. Although the lead crime-scene technician will be hammered during the trial for performing their job poorly, it always comes back to the lead investigator. Therefore, an investigator should know which methods are used for packaging and storing evidence. They should take into account the size of the evidence being stored and does the storage facility have the space. There are times when evidence such as vehicles, doors, or other large items are collected, if the facility in the respective police department cannot store these items, then a cost will be incurred if another facility needs to be used.

As the processing of the crime scene winds down, the investigator assigned to supervise the crime-scene processing must confer with the lead crime-scene technician and go over everything that has been done to that point. Investigators need to do a final walk-through of the crime scene, observe the evidence cones and placards, determine if anything else needs to be done at the scene before releasing the scene. Remember, once the crime scene is released, evidence lost cannot be replaced.

In conclusion, investigators need to make sure that all evidence is documented and photographed before being collected. They must write in their notepads the types of evidence that was located, things such as tool markings, trace evidence, G.S.R. or D.N.A., and confer with the lead crime-scene technician as to how these items were collected and packaged. It is vital for the investigator and the crime-scene technician to be on the same page. Sometimes, investigators take the crime-scene personnel for granted and this is a grave error. Once a good professional working relationship is established between them, the results are endless because everyone takes ownership of the case being investigated. Knowledge is powerful and every investigator should have an understanding of the responsibilities that crime-scene technicians have and what they are capable of processing at a crime scene. This chapter is geared toward making an investigator have a better understanding of the crime scene and what can be done, not to make them crime-scene technicians.

Chapter 3
Notifying the Medical Examiner and State Attorney

Every death investigation is assigned to a lead investigator. All investigative teams assign a lead investigator as the primary, and the other team members are assigned responsibilities that will assist the lead investigator throughout the course of the investigation. Usually, the lead investigator remains on the scene long enough to gather information needed, before leaving to either conduct interviews of witnesses or contact living victim(s) in the hospital. There may be additional crimes scenes that need to be examined which will need the lead investigator's attention. Once the lead investigator has determined what course of action they will take, whether to remain on the scene or leave, someone from the investigative team must remain at the scene to wait for the medical examiner and the on-call state attorney.

Previously, the crime scene was discussed from the perspective of identifying and documenting evidence, the relationship between the lead investigator and the lead crime-scene technician. Now, the investigation is geared toward working closely with the state attorney's office (prosecutors) and the medical examiner (coroner). During this phase, the team in-charge of the investigation makes contact with the on-call state attorney and medical examiner. They will advise the investigator what the estimated time of arrival (E.T.A.) will be. There are occasions when the wait can be several hours and there are times when neither entity responds to the scene. Nonetheless, notifications must be made to the on-call medical examiner. The investigator must consider, if a *search warrant* (this will be discussed in the state-attorney section) will be needed, then additional time will be spent at the crime scene.

Once an estimated time of arrival is given, this allows the investigative team to continue working with the crime-scene technician until the medical examiner arrives. Remember, the crime scene is still active and the victim (decedent) that is in the scene is an important part of the crime scene. Throughout these pages, decedent will be referred to as victim. The crime scene should remain secured from unauthorized personnel entering or exiting the crime scene. This continues to be the responsibility of the lead investigator. Although this is an active crime scene, the victim is not disturbed until the medical examiner arrives on the scene. The reason is as follows; the medical examiner, upon arrival on the scene, wants to view the victim and take photographs of the scene as it was found. They want to confer with the lead investigator and crime-scene technician in order to discuss measurements of the scene and note the meteorological conditions.

Prior to the medical examiner beginning their on-scene examination, they will brief with the lead investigator and lead crime-scene technician. This meeting enables both the medical examiner and the investigator to engage in a collegial relationship that promotes interagency rapport. During this briefing, the medical examiner will be given a brief synopsis surrounding the incident. Additionally, it allows for a clear exchange of ideas which can assist in solving the case.

Afterwards, assignments will be given to whomever is tasked to assist the medical examiner with the on-scene examination of the victim.

The responsibility of the crime-scene technician, during this phase, is to photograph, document, and collect any item(s) of evidentiary value found on the victim. During this stage of the on-scene examination, the victim's clothing is examined and removed, leaving the victim naked on the scene. This procedure seems unthoughtful, but it is extremely necessary and is done with the utmost respect for the victim. During this phase of the on-scene examination, wounds such as gunshots, cuts, punctures, blunt-force trauma, and other injuries or defects are noted, documented, and photographed. This examination is performed so that the medical examiner can determine what areas of the body are to be x-rayed. Some of those items can be trace evidence or clothing, but when clothes are saturated with blood or other fluids, they will go with the victim to the medical examiner's office and placed in a drying room. A scribe will be assigned to assist the crime-scene technician as well as the lead investigator, regarding everything that is done, processed, collected, or sent to another location must be documented in order to maintain accountability of what was done while examining the victim.

Once the on-scene examination of the victim is completed, the removal services unit will respond to the crime scene, tag the victim, secure the victim inside a plastic bag, and place the victim inside the transport van. The victim will be transported to the medical examiner's office and a date and time for the postmortem examination will be given by the medical examiner. Prior to the victim being removed from the scene or before the lead investigator ends his tour of duty; a medical examiner sheet (initial report of the incident) will be completed and taken to the medical examiner's office. This report gives a short synopsis of the incident and includes the victim's information and next of kin (N.O.K.) information. This is entered in the report so that the medical examiner's investigator can contact the family for legal identification of the victim.

Once the medical examiner confirms the date and time for the postmortem examination of the victim, the lead investigator or his designee will attend. In order to become a thorough and competent investigator, it is suggested to attend as many postmortems as possible and get to know the different medical examiners or fellows that perform these examinations. During this part of an investigation, copious notes should be taken and every question imaginable should be asked. As an aspiring investigator, make it a point to attend any of the Medicolegal or Death Investigation courses that are available. The information obtained during these courses are immeasurable and the contacts that are made with investigators from agencies across the state and country is very valuable.

All investigators start their careers hoping to become the next Sherlock Holmes and think that a violent crime, such as a homicide, can be solved in no time. This is far from the truth; it takes dedication, sacrifice, and a willingness to go the extra mile. Review the details in the section, 'Mental Preparation,' it should give the investigator a better perspective of what it takes.

The relationship between the investigator and the medical examiner is crucial. The medical examiner will be subpoenaed to testify at hearings and trial, so they must be well versed in your investigation in order for them to provide the most accurate testimony based on the physical evidence. Let us proceed as to what the responsibilities are for the medical examiner as well as the lead investigator. Keep in mind, an investigator investigates and a medical examiner performs the postmortem of the victim. The medical examiner's investigation is independent to that of the homicide investigator. Medical examiners are doctors, investigators are not, but both work closely together. Investigators have a responsibility to understand terminologies, anatomy, and a basic understanding of what makes humans function and what can cause them to stop functioning.

Investigators are not medical examiners, nor should they believe that some training in this field makes them experts. Investigators will be exposed to terminologies such as cause of death and manner of death, terminologies to which they must be familiar. Types of death that appear in the medical examiner report can be natural, unclassified, accidental, suicide, or homicide. So, let us visit a part of what an investigator will be asked to know from the medicolegal standpoint. Aspects of death investigations have varied components, which we are going to view. When discussing homicide investigations, legal terminology and aspects of the investigation will be covered in the State-Attorney section of this chapter.

In the early stages of my investigative career, it was my privilege to associate myself with accomplished forensic pathologists such as the late Chief Medical Examiner Joseph H. Davis M.D. (for whom the Miami-Dade Medical Examiners building is named after), Associate Medical Examiners Valerie J. Rao, M.D., the late Bruce Hyma M.D., and Emma O. Lew, M.D., whom I have had the pleasure of working closely with during the past 25 years. The relationships forged with these great doctors furthered my interest in how to properly investigate violent crimes, namely *Homicide.*

Florida State Statute 406, Medical Examiner; governs the rules and duties under specific sub-statutes, authority, and guidelines by which medical examiners perform their duties.

It is a well-known fact that a pathologist ignorant of the case background and the investigative methods used by the lead police investigator is of little or no value, and may hinder or mislead the investigation. Therefore, it is vital for the lead investigator to conduct the on-scene investigation thoroughly (as noted in the Crime Scene chapter) and gather as much information as possible which will assist the medical examiner when they conduct the postmortem examination. As an investigator, they have a responsibility to reconstruct how an incident took place, present the facts to the medical examiner, and allow them to interpret how death occurred by the physical examination and laboratory results.

The lead investigator, working closely with the medical examiner, must have an understanding of the causation of death. There are the human factors, mechanical factors, and environmental factors related to *all* death investigations. Within these factors, there are subsets which will be viewed and examined independently. During the course of every investigation, investigators need to understand that there is a *pre-event, event,* and *post-event.* These terms are related to each incident, independently. The *pre-event* are factors that occur prior to an incident-taking place, such as a verbal altercation between a subject and a victim. Then you have the *event* itself, where the subject decides to take out a handgun from their waistband and discharge the handgun. Then there is the *post-event,* where the victim sustains a gunshot wound or gunshot wounds that cause injuries resulting in death.

Investigative principles that a homicide investigator must be familiar with are as previously stated, manner of death. The lead investigator needs to know that manner means, a way of doing something or the way in which a thing is done or takes place. How is manner of death classified? The lead investigator in any death investigation must know that classifications are as follows; *manner* of *death* refers to natural disease or unnatural. During any death investigation where unnatural death is discussed, the investigative team knows the various classifications and which way they can steer an investigation. These are accidental, suicide, homicide, and unclassified. On rare occasions, the medical examiner might classify an incident as undetermined. When discussing *cause* of *death,* one must revert to the meaning of cause, which is something that produces an effect, result, or consequence. Dr. Lester Adelson of the Cuyahoga County Coroner's office, Cleveland, Ohio, determined that, "The cause of death is the injury, disease, or the combination of the two responsible for initiating the train of physiological disturbances, briefed or prolonged, which produced the fatal termination." Another term that will be viewed later is m*echanism* of *death.* Mechanism is viewed as the physiological derangement or biochemical disturbance incompatible with life which is initiated by the *cause of death*. Mechanisms of death include hemorrhage, metabolic disturbances, ventricular fibrillation, respiratory depression, or profound sepsis. There are others that can be covered during a medicolegal training.

There are ways in which an investigation is conducted that can determine the medical examiner's outcome. The following is an example:

1. Terminal event.
2. Environment.
3. Medical history.

4. Any additional historical information.
5. Hypothesis of event (mechanism(s) and cause).
6. Evidence gathered at scene and autopsy should have an investigative correlation.
7. Hypothesis is confirmed/denied.
8. Additional questions, if needed.

The evidence gathered by the investigator is crucial to the medical examiner. Based on what is learned at the scene and autopsy, the medical examiner can formulate with *degree* of *certainty* what the cause and manner of death was. The medical examiner, as the investigators on any investigation, when using the terminology describing *proof*, should use terms such as 'evidence of' as opposed to 'prove.'

As an investigator, you cannot use opinion to formulate the case. The investigator can opine in order to gather thoughts and possible motives or suspects, but not to use it as concrete proof. On the other hand, the medical examiner, as an expert, uses opinion in different stages. *Possible* is less than 50%. *Probable* is 51%. *Clear* and *convincing* is 75%. To the exclusion of any and all reasonable doubt is 95% and *absolute certainty* is 100%. These percentages are mostly used by attorneys (prosecutors or defense) assigned to the case, since medical examiners rarely use such terms. The conclusion of an investigation that equates to reasonable medical certainty or probability is given a value higher than probable. However, that conclusion is made by the medical examiner and an investigator should have the working relationship with the medical examiner assigned to the incident, to consult with the medical examiner and have an understanding as to the thought process behind the conclusion.

Any additional evidence that is gathered goes a long way in corroborating evidence already obtained by the investigator or the medical examiner. Additional evidence increases the degree of certainty by which a case will be determined. The investigator must keep in mind that additional facts or evidence can also alter the conclusion of the medical examiner if the additional facts do not line up with what was originally learned. An investigator's responsibility is to be as thorough as possible during the investigation and should always include the medical examiner in any briefings that might affect the outcome of the medical examiner's conclusion. A homicide investigator is not a medical examiner. However, investigators should attend training that will assist them in understanding the role of the medical examiner and how investigations are affected.

Various Types of Death Cases, Starting with Cardiac

The following are types of death that can become murder. For example, how a sudden cardiac arrest can be determined or classified as a murder. Should it be? There are cases where this type of event can be classified as a murder. An investigator needs to understand that not all non-traumatic deaths that occur during a felony should be considered a murder. Investigators must be careful in charging murder under this circumstance when causational evidence is insufficient. "Criminal responsibility for manslaughter should be determined by considering all of the surrounding circumstances, and not from considering the result alone." This finding was from a 1965 case, William Joseph Penton vs. State of Florida. During this incident, not all of the surrounding circumstances were considered before going to trial. The medical examiner's report, in this case and other cases, should be considered before an investigator considers charging a subject with murder. In instances where the possibility exist that a murder charge will be applied, the investigator must consider the final report of the medical examiner before consultation with the state attorney assigned to the case.

In sudden cardiac deaths, Dr. Joseph H. Davis, M.D., and Dr. Ronald K. Wright, M.D., surmised that; sudden unexpected death usually involves one of two mechanisms, fast heart stoppage or slow heart stoppage with respiratory arrest. These physiological derangements arise from diverse causes that are sometimes purely functional without structural correlates. The autopsy is only considered an investigative tool to be employed and is interpreted in the light of the terminal event, social and medical history, and environmental circumstances.

Social and medical history of a victim lend themselves to how an investigator can consider charging a suspect with murder. A victim of an armed robbery suddenly collapses to the floor during the commission of the robbery without having been injured. In order for the investigator to charge the suspect with murder, they must consider the above stated factors to determine if the victim was in fear during the event, as well as wait for the results of the autopsy. This example of the victim collapsing could be from a sudden heart failure. Therefore, the investigator must consult with the attending medical examiner to determine sub-factors such as drug use or metabolic diseases. Lifestyles of victims along with the environment tend to give clarity of how the victims comported themselves and did these factors play a part in the sudden death and not the felonious event.

When investigators respond to a scene of a *drowning death* (a.k.a. floater), a person who was found in a body of water such as a pool, bathtub, toilets/buckets (mainly young children), lakes, canals, oceans, or any type of liquid. Drowning is defined as submersion in a liquid. Death by drowning is caused by the lack of oxygen to the brain. Although drowning deaths are relatively uncommon considering the numerous bodies of water around Florida, one is still too many. There are other terms occasionally used, such as *near drowning* and *dry drowning*. One refers to a victim that survives more than 24 hours after a drowning experience occurred, but other factors should be taken into consideration. Then, you find that the second event which is believed to occur in 10-15% of drowning incidents. In short, this incident takes place when small amount of water is inhaled into the blood stream during the perimortem phase. These two types of drowning require extensive study that would occur during a medicolegal course conducted by the local medical examiner's office. Investigators must understand that investigating a death by drowning is extremely challenging. The investigation of the scene can be difficult due to many factors associated with the location and environment; the investigation must be conducted with extra caution not to dismiss foul play. Investigators should understand that in the United States, roughly 10 deaths occur daily from drowning, and one in five victims of drowning are children under the age of 14. In addition, African Americans and Native Americans have a higher chance of drowning than Caucasians. Other factors to consider are that of a medical episode that leads to the terminal event. While at the scene, the investigator should note the position of the victim, a very classic position is the head down, buttocks up, and all extremities dangling. As part of the investigation, investigators should request information regarding water current, and if low or high tide played a factor. An investigator may come across a drowning victim that was submerged for an extended period, but due to natural gases in the body, the victim floated to the surface. In various parts of the country where water conditions are colder or water freezes, victims can be found months after the terminal event took place. *It* is important for the investigator and the medical examiner to carefully examine all of the factors before a cause and manner of death is given. These cases are usually given the title of *unclassified,* until the results from toxicology test, medical history, additional laboratory test, and autopsy are examined.

During an apparent drowning investigation, the investigative collaboration between the investigator and the medical examiner goes a long way in assisting the medical examiner to determine the cause and manner of death. One needs to understand that a mass in an advance stage of decomposition, found in a body of water is not always a human body or parts of a human. At times, the mass may be anything from a pig to a goat. In any case, all of the evidence is documented, collected, and transported to the medical examiner's office for further examination. Based on the circumstances, a medical examiner might respond to the scene in order to get a firsthand view. This will assist them in making a final determination and to uncover if the mass was indeed human or animal. Bodies recovered from water lend themselves to various challenges such as slippage of the epidermis or additional wounds that are caused by animal. These wounds must be documented and examined closely to determine if they are postmortem or ante-mortem injuries. The longer the body has been in the water, the more deformities can be associated with the length of time in the water.

Investigators, in cases such as these, must ensure that documentation is extremely detailed and the scene processing is conducted in a methodical manner to ensure that no additional evidence is lost. Remember, findings during the autopsy, along with a timeline of the victim and medical/social history and other factors, will give the medical examiner what is needed to pronounce the cause and manner of death. Many times, investigators submit apparent human remains to the medical examiner's office for examination that turn up to be something other than human. However, an investigator must error on the side of caution and if in doubt, contact the on-call medical examiner and explain the circumstances surrounding the incident and they will be more than happy to assist. There may come a time when a SCUBA diver is a victim of an apparent drowning. Many additional factors come into play when investigating such an incident. Heart disease can play a part in such cases, an embolism, and even running out of air. The investigator must also consider equipment failure, such as regulator, compass, and even the scuba tank. Many tests have to be performed regarding the scuba tanks in order to eliminate doubt. Too many factors go into developing a cause and manner of death and in many occasions, the medical examiner's findings take months.

Deaths caused because of fire are investigated to the fullest, like any other death investigation, fire fatalities pose various challenges during the investigative phase. In the United States, thousands of victims die because of fires. Many of the cases are accidental in nature and can be attributed to careless smoking, faulty electrical equipment, unattended stoves, children playing with matches, and many more. During the course of a death by fire investigation, victims that are impaired such as children, elderly, and abusers of alcohol as well as drugs, seem to be the ones that are most at risk. The majority of the death investigations that I have been involved with, regarding fire deaths, involved either unattended candles, electrical wires that were old, or mattress catching fire from burning cigarette. In discussing the mechanism of fire deaths, investigators must understand that many victims have a different timetable of death based on the types of injuries sustained during the initial event. Investigators will come across cases where the victim lives days, weeks, and even months before they succumb to their injuries. In such cases, death is a result of the body going into shock, smoke inhalation, or burns. Usually, sepsis or respiratory failure is the mechanism of death. A vast majority of the cases in which I have been involved with, death was a result of smoke inhalation. *Smoke inhalation* is usually the cause of death instead of burns; carbon monoxide is the mark used by the medical examiner during these cases. Carbon monoxide is detected in the blood system and the levels will not rise after death. During a fire, if a victim were breathing, they would have inhaled soot or other debris. Investigators need to carefully examine the victim and look for indicators such as residue associated with soot around the mouth and nose. The medical examiner can examine other aspects of soot when the postmortem is performed. There are many other aspects pertaining to smoke inhalation that can be explained in greater details when investigators attend any medicolegal course.

Investigators must be careful during the scene investigation and the on-scene physical examination of the victim, to document abnormalities such as blistering, scalding burns, and even the victim's clothing, materials around the area, to determine if the fire was intentionally set. Another type of burning is a chemical burn which can be identified by the pattern it leaves on the victim. When liquid splashes, the investigator can see the pattern on the victim's body or clothing. These chemical burns are usually associated in warehouses or any place where chemicals are stored. In few cases, an investigator may come across a victim of a suicide that has ingested liquids like Drano or Clorox. At these scenes, it is important for the investigator to brief the medical examiner of what has been discovered.

Investigators come across fatalities caused by electrocution. *Electrical deaths* are mainly caused by amperage, which is the amount of current that flows through a victim's body. Many of the electrical deaths that I have investigated dealt with victims cutting trees, attempting to get mangoes or avocados. In many of these cases, the victims reached up with a pole that made contact with power lines. In doing so, the higher voltage ran through low resistance which creates a greater shock. In these cases, the investigator needs to examine the victim for subtle evidence that they were electrocuted. The victim should have a burn at the point of contact or exit. Meaning, the point of entrance is where the electrical voltage entered the victim and the exit point is where the current cleared the victim to reach the ground. Investigators need to understand that there are other types of deaths related to thermal injuries, these can be investigated and studied while attending Medicolegal or Death Investigation courses. Investigators must also consider that death from electrocution can be from high or low voltage.

The role played by the lead investigator and crime-scene technician is crucial in assisting the medical examiner to determine the cause and manner of death associated with a fire or burns. Thorough documentation, processing, and collecting of evidence is of great value to the medical examiner, along with the notes taken by the lead investigator and arson investigator. Nothing in a crime scene can be overlooked or taken for granted. *Most importantly, when dealing with any type of electrical fatality, investigators must ensure that all power is turned off before entering a scene.*

The lead investigator needs to keep in mind the possibility of the incident being a murder. Thereby making sure and considering any abnormality in the death scene. As part of the investigation, the primary agency will assign an arson investigator to the homicide team. In addition, the state-fire Marshall may be included if the primary agency does not have an Arson Investigator. The lead investigator should consider many factors during the initial stages of a death resulting from a fire or burns. These factors must be shared with the medical examiner assigned to the case in order for them to make the proper determination as to the cause and manner of death.

The investigator, along with the medical examiner, must examine what was the causation of the fire or burn death. There are several factors, such as human error, environmental and equipment/mechanical. During the course of the investigation, several questions must be answered. Where did the fire start and how? In what manner did the fire spread? Where was the victim found in relationship to where the victim was prior to the fire starting? Who were the witnesses and what information did they provide? What were the victim's social, economic, and medical histories? The scene investigation is crucial in order to answer these questions or at least, to have a better understanding that will assist in clearing the case.

During the course of a fire or burn investigation, the correlation between the physical evidence and the witness accounts are vital and an integral part of the investigation. The deliberate manner in which the lead investigator and others assigned to the incident examines the crime scene is a vital component that can determine the outcome. Nothing during the initial stages of the scene investigation can go unnoticed or undocumented. It is precisely this information that can assist in interpreting what and how the incident took place. For the lead investigator, factors that need to be examined are, was the victim sleeping and if so, was the victim smoking. If the victim was in an area filled with combustible material, did that material accelerate the fire that caused the death? If there was, an explosion associated with the fire, what material(s) was near the victim when the explosion occurred. It is important to note that as a lead investigator, their responsibility is to complete a thorough search of the scene and to interview all possible witnesses that can assist with the investigation. The lead investigator is not an arson investigator and they should allow those with a specific expertise to conduct their investigation in correlation with the death investigation. There are aspects of a fire caused by an explosion that not all investigators can determine. However, investigators must understand that fires caused by an explosion can arise from a chemical event (the result of chemical interactions, resulting in space-occupying gases) to a meteoritic event (not common, but meteors that consist of tiny fragments that burn up due to atmospheric friction). Ultimately, as briefings take place between all of the various entities and experts assigned to the case, a clear picture can be made for how and why the fire materialized. The final cause of death is up to the pathologist once they have received the police and arson investigator's findings of their investigation. These results can take months.

I have thoughtfully tried to inform the fledgling investigator of the various types of death investigations. From many years of experience, I can assure you, you might not investigate every type of death case. However, an investigator must be familiar with each type of death case in the event that such a case is assigned to them. *An investigator's responsibility is to be thorough and complete. Slow and methodical, not fast and sloppy.* An investigator that truly wishes to make death investigations their profession must attend as many lectures and certified trainings as possible. These various types of tutorials can only make the investigator better.

Now, let us continue on this journey. Most of the following death cases are cases in which I have closely investigated or in one way been associated. Nevertheless, this is not about war stories, this continues to be about the relationship between the lead investigator and the medical examiner. The way in which they each investigate a death case and how final cause and manner of death is determined.

Homicide investigative units around the country are assigned to investigate natural deaths daily. These cases range in scope from a heart attack to a complex illness. Being assigned such a case is no different than investigating a homicide. The basic premise is the same; an investigator must control, secure, and document the death scene. This is not to say that the scene is as intense as a violent scene, but the investigator must be as meticulous. These cases are how new investigators receive their training. In order to move on to a more complex investigation, a junior investigator must demonstrate that they are proficient in investigating the less-stressful cases. These are the cases where the junior investigator learns how to do an on-scene physical examination of a deceased victim to ensure that no foul play has been committed. Investigators are hands on and begin to understand why copious amounts of notes are so necessary. On these scenes, documentation of medicines is crucial to learning the medical history of the victim. Interviewing the next of kin, friends, or witnesses go a long way in determining what the victim's last moves were before the fatal event.

So, let us understand that a natural death is not caused by an accident, suicide, or homicide. Instead, a natural death is one related to a specific type of disease. As an investigator, it is rare to be involved with exotic diseases, there are so many that one cannot keep up. The Center for Disease Control is a great source of information if one of these rare diseases are encountered. However, let us concentrate on the most common. Investigators normally respond to natural death cases caused by a disease that debilitates or quickly kills a victim that, up to the moment of death, appeared to be in good physical condition. Heart disease or some type of congenital heart diseases can cause these deaths. Additionally, epilepsy, asthma, pulmonary thromboembolism, or the sudden rupturing of diseased arteries may cause death. In children, Sudden Infant Death Syndrome (S.I.D.S.) for a long time was associated with natural deaths, but in recent years, this train of thought has changed. The Miami-Dade Medical Examiner's Office makes sure that one of their investigators respond to the scenes where children have died and based on the information they receive from the lead investigator and an on-scene reenactment with the next of kin. In many cases, these deaths become one of asphyxia. Homicide of a child by strangulation or suffocation is not common, so in more cases than not, a child found dead is most likely to be from a natural or accidental cause. However, the lead investigator cannot discount the possibility of homicide. This is where the on-scene investigation, along with the interviews of witnesses, become crucial.

Other death investigations that a junior investigator will encounter are the ones associated with victims that are living a lifestyle not conducive to healthy living. These victims suffer from diseases such as alcoholism, drug addictions, and some sort of mental illness and the complications that manifest themselves.

Of these natural death cases, in my experience, the most common death case that an investigator will come across is the *heart attack.* A heart attack that leads to the victim's death is caused by a sudden rhythm change of the heart. This change leads to a lack of blood flowing to the brain. Another type is cardiac rhythm; this is when electrical impulses of the heart malfunction, causing the muscle to contract and expulsion of blood. This can be a result of arteriosclerosis or atherosclerosis, which is when the arteries are narrowed and blood has a difficult time flowing. This sudden decrease of blood flow causes the particular heart muscle to die from a lack of blood. There are many factors that determine why arteriosclerosis forms, this, I leave to the medical profession. Nevertheless, it is important, as I have stated previously, for an investigator to have a general understanding of what they are investigating.

The investigator's role, during this type of investigation, is to gather all of the particular historical information of the victim prior to the fatal event. In the majority of these cases, an investigator is able to contact the victim's attending physician that can give light to the victim's medical history. A check of the victim's prescription drugs goes a long way in gathering what the medical history is. Interviewing those who were present or had contact with the victim prior to death can lend to physical condition prior to death. If the primary-care physician is not available and does not return the investigator's call, then the medical examiner will be notified. If this becomes a medical examiner's case, it is important that whatever medications were at the scene, they must be submitted to the medical examiner's office with the victim. In these type cases, the medical examiner will contact the victim's physician or review the victim's medical history, medication(s), and determine the cause and manner of death. If the victim has no medical history or attending physician, then an autopsy may be warranted, but that is a decision made by the medical examiner. For this reason, it is crucial for the lead investigator to document and inform the medical examiner of what was learned at the scene, this information is crucial.

As previously noted, the junior investigator must treat a natural death as if it were a homicide. Consistency throughout every investigation allows mistakes to be minimal, preferably non-existent. Therefore, the processing of the scene by the crime-scene technician, the interviewing of witnesses, speaking with the primary physician who can advise of the victim's medical history and if it correlates with the victim's illness. Medications at the scene, along with the victim's position and the on-scene physical examination, needs to be documented. In performing the on-scene physical examination, the investigator is looking for keys such as bruising or defects to the body, bleeding or marks that are not common. It is important to understand the type of illness the witnesses describe, such as 'heart disease,' 'high blood pressure,' 'diabetes,' or 'hypertension.' The terminal event must be described if seen, and are the medications at the scene consistent with the victim's medical history. The investigator needs to keep in mind the remote possibility of suicide or accidental death from overdose. Also, when speaking with the primary physician, ask questions that are relevant to the investigation. Make sure that the primary physician has been attending the victim for a period of time and feels comfortable in signing the death certificate. Summarizing the above, it is important to treat each natural death investigation as if it were a homicide. The investigator must be consistent concerning documentation, scene processing, and interviewing witnesses. They must also speak with the victim's primary physician and gather a medical history which would be consistent with the terminal event. Ascertain if the primary physician feels comfortable in signing the death certificate, if not, the victim must be transported to the medical examiner's office along with the medications located at the scene in order, for the medical examiner, assigned to the case, to determine cause and manner of death.

Another common case investigated by the homicide unit are unclassified deaths or accidental deaths. These cases are the next level of training for the young investigator. Once the investigator feels comfortable investigating natural death cases, the unclassified death case is the next step in the training phase. During the evolution of a homicide investigator, like any other profession, investigators must feel comfortable with each evolution. Therefore, investigating unclassified deaths is no different than investigating a homicide. However, in order to feel confident investigating a homicide, investigators must be extremely proficient while investigating less stressful, but, yet important cases. Therefore, an investigator has just arrived at their first unclassified death scene. How does the approach differ from investigating a natural death?

In reality, it does not. The investigator must follow the same steps taken at the natural case. The slight variation in this investigation may be that the victim has no primary physician or negative medical history. The victim may be young and the socioeconomic status may or may not play a part in the death. Nevertheless, investigators must conduct witness interviews that can give a timeline of the final moments prior to the terminal event. The death scene must be thoroughly processed and all evidence documented and collected. The lead investigator must call the on-call medical examiner in the event that they want to respond to the death scene. The investigator must conduct the on-scene physical examination of the victim, head to toe, in order to eliminate any possibility of trauma having been inflicted on the victim. Location of where the victim is found plays a big factor in putting the pieces together. Once the investigator concludes the on-scene investigation and it has been determined that the victim will be transported to the medical examiner's office, a briefing between the investigator and the medical examiner assigned to the case must be had. The investigator must pass on as much information as possible to the medical examiner, this will assist greatly in determining the cause and manner of death. Anytime there is a sudden death by a victim that by all accounts is healthy, questions are asked that need to be answered. The terminal event could be a result of an undetected illness or caused by an event which was self-induced, such as a drug overdose or poison. There is also the possibility of suicide and that is why the victim's social history is important. Therefore, based on the investigator's thorough investigation and the collaboration with the medical examiner, the chances of determining a cause and manner of death improves. In my experience, these cases can take up, too, several months to complete, mainly because toxicology tests and results have to be analyzed. Ultimately, the vast majority of these cases are classified as natural or accidental. The contributing factors can be from an undetected illness to an accidental mixture of medications. The investigator's responsibility is to consult with the medical examiner in order to gather the information needed for the lead investigator to author the final supplemental report.

Blunt force trauma is a type of injury that an investigator will observe on a victim during the course of a violent incident. These types of cases are common and must be closely examined and investigated, from the criminal and medicolegal aspect. As previously discussed, the collaboration between the investigator and the medical examiner is paramount. While investigating incidents of blunt force trauma, investigators have an obligation to understand the classification and pattern recognition of the injuries. These, along with the three categories of blunt force trauma, are important for the lead investigator to understand, if they are to properly communicate with the medical examiner. Although we are discussing blunt force trauma from a criminal aspect, which could result in death, investigators should be able to differentiate blunt force trauma that might have occurred from an automobile accident, a physical confrontation (fight), or any fall from an extended height, either accidentally or by design. It is important for the lead investigator to inform the medical examiner the type of injuries sustained and circumstances involved with the incident. Knowledge of the type of blunt force trauma sustained is important to how the investigation will proceed.

Blunt-force-trauma injuries are defined as injuries that occur when the body violently strikes against a blunt object or when the blunt object impacts the body. These impacts cause bruising to the body's tissues. An investigator should be able to distinguish between blunt-force-trauma injuries and sharp-force-trauma injuries. These types of injuries are discernable and an investigator must be able to articulate each. The investigator needs to know that blunt-force-trauma injuries are the tearing of tissues, crushing of tissues, and even as simple as scraping. There are *three categories* related to blunt force trauma, which are; *Lacerations* (knife fight), *Abrasions* (fall or being dragged), and *Contusions* (punch, strike from blunt object).

When the medical examiner discusses *lacerations,* the investigator must know and understand that a laceration is defined as the tearing, splitting, or crushing which causes injuries to a victim from blunt force. Investigators must comprehend that lacerations cause defects to the skin, soft tissue, or internal organs. During the course of the initial on-scene physical examination of the victim, investigators' observations are critical in distinguishing a laceration from a sharp-force injury. Lacerations can be distinguished from cuts to the skin. Cuts and lacerations are most notable to have deep wounds where tissues, nerves, and blood vessels are exposed. These wounds are called incised wounds. The direction of a wound can assist the investigator in knowing which way the force was applied. In such wounds, the deepest part of the wound lets the investigator know the final resting place of the object used to cause such a wound and the force applied. The appearance of wounds caused by laceration can differ. The investigator should be able to describe what they observe to the medical examiner and understand what the medical examiner is describing to them during the physical examination. In addition, surfaces play a big role in how wounds can look.

Many of the internal injuries that I have observed throughout my career are that of pancreas, stomach, small intestine, and mostly the liver. According to the various medical examiners that have spoken to these injuries, they express that the compression of the organ between the offending force and the vertebral column causes such injuries. These injuries are best studied during a medicolegal lecture or by attending an autopsy related to such an injury. When an investigator describes the injuries, the total amount of wounds counts toward interpreting the impacts sustained by the victim, such as; if a victim sustained four lacerations, five abrasions, and five contusions, then the total number of impacts is fourteen. Now, there is a possibility of secondary wounds caused by the initial event. A victim might have fallen during the course of the terminal event and fractured a bone or had additional abrasions, these are wounds caused consequent to the event. Blunt-force-trauma injuries, which are observed on the nose, hips, knees, elbows, back of head, or forehead, can be attributed to the victim falling because these are areas that are normally impacted during a fall.

What the investigator learns at such a scene will determine how the investigation will proceed. If, during the course of an investigation, the investigator or medical examiner discover bruising/injuries to parts of the body that are not normally exposed, these are injuries that need to be explained. Thus, the possibility of foul play must be explored.

Multiplane injury should raise an investigator's suspicion, especially when they occur on the head. The more injuries that are observed around the plain surface of the head, the less likely that the victim just fell while standing. These types of injuries are observed when the victim was pummeled by an assailant or on a child that has been beaten, as opposed to just falling.

I have not investigated many deaths as a result of jumping from heights, but I have been part of homicide teams that have. One of the observations made in such cases are, that injuries caused by a fall in and of itself, which causes death, cannot determine if the fall was intentional or accidental. The height from which the victim fell will determine the type of injury patterns sustained. Injuries which can be observed from victims that fall from extensive heights can be heel fractures, shattered legs (tibia/fibula), fractured vertebrae, and fractured skull. One very rare event is when an object strikes the chest area with such force that causes the heart to stop. This event is called Commotio Cordis. In all of my years as an investigator, I learned of one such incident which occurred during a softball game. A third baseman ran toward the plate at precisely the time when the batter struck the ball, sending it directly at the third baseman. The ball struck the third baseman on the chest and with great force, at which time he immediately collapsed and was pronounced deceased on the scene by fire rescue. This is the only time I ever heard of such an incident.

All investigators must feel comfortable understanding, identifying, and explaining what blunt force trauma is. The ability to explain such injuries to the medical examiner goes a long way in how the investigation will proceed. As the medical examiner conducts the postmortem examination, they will be able to explain the injuries to the investigator in detail and the investigator will be able to observe the injuries that occurred internally. These are the moments in which the investigators need to ask questions that will assist them in future investigations. The investigator's notes are crucial in order to present the best information to the medical examiner. As in all notes, they should be accurate and consistent.

When dealing with *abrasions,* the investigator has to know that these injuries are caused by friction or rubbing against an object that causes a superficial injury to the skin. These injuries are anything from scratches, scrapes, grazes, or burn marks (not from fire). Scratches are abrasions that can be caused by fingernails, tree branch, fence, or a corner of a concrete wall. A scrape or graze is a wider abrasion. Patterned abrasions are injuries that reflect distinct characteristics of the surface that impacted against the victim. These types of patterns can be tire marks (treads) or pattern from shoes (like the sneaker imprints in the Mercado case). Ligature marks are most noted in such cases, as suicide by hanging or what the medical examiners call, ligature strangulation (murder). When a victim is struck or dragged by a vehicle or any other type of machinery, this can cause friction abrasion (skin burns) injuries. These injuries are seen more in traffic-homicide incidents as opposed to murder cases. There are instances when victims are intentionally run down, where these type injuries are observed (Esther Longo case M.P.D. homicide 82/83). The lead investigator, in examining the crime scene and when performing the on-scene physical examination of the victim, must note how the victim was dressed. Was the victim wearing heavy clothing? Heavy clothing can prevent injuries from being prominent, even if the cause was from a forceful impact.

There are incidents where an investigator will respond to which the victim is found deceased with what appears to be multiple abrasion-type injuries. In many cases, the victim had been deceased for an unknown period of time or physically disabled prior to the terminal event. In such cases, during the physical examination of the victim, the investigator should understand that there is the possibility that animals might have begun to eat the victim. Insects, ants, and cockroaches often bite the victim. These bites can be mistaken for abrasions and this is called anthropophagy. These types of injuries, when examined closely, are without bleeding or inflammation. Elderly victims can suffer injuries associated from immobility. They are always in the same position, which cause skin sores. Mostly, these injuries are to the back of the victim's (head/spine). Investigators should understand that postmortem abrasions can occur and are identified because the injuries do not bleed or have inflammation. These injuries can have diverse coloration such as yellow, red, or light brown.

When discussing *contusions* with regards to homicide or violent crimes investigations, the lead investigator should understand that this type of injury is caused by blunt force. The blunt force exerted creates damage to the deep parts of the skin, which allows for blood vessels and blood seeping into the tissue. This injury causes the dark blue, purple/blue discoloration in the area of the injury. These types of injuries cause bruises or hematomas and often occur prior to the terminal event. These injuries are often observed during a violent confrontation in domestic violence cases. An investigator, during the investigation where contusions are present, should make sure when interviewing witnesses or victim(s) that they ascertain what degree of force was used. In addition, what type of weapon (blunt object or other) did the assailant use? Investigators need to understand that if great force applied on a victim, in a small area of the body, the greater likelihood that the bruise will be larger. The location of the contusion, along with the age of the victim, are factors that an investigator needs to take into account. Remember, older victims have fragile skin and bruise easier than young, virile victims. Victims that are taking blood-thinner medication have a greater chance of showing a larger section of bruising. These contusions are caused with less force applied. For a homicide investigator, the size of the bruise can be a good indicator of how long the victim survived prior to death. An investigator must remember that so long as the victim is alive, blood is still flowing/circulating into the area of tissue damage. In death investigations where a child is punched or kicked, the initial crime-scene investigation may not show any contusions to the victim(s) body. It will not be until the postmortem is performed that bruising will be evident to regions of the belly and damage to internal organs. During the course of a child's death investigation, physical evidence and the interviews of witnesses are paramount in order to establish what occurred prior to the terminal event. This information is crucial to the medical examiner and in most incidents, they will dispatch a reconstruction investigator to the scene to conduct interviews and possible reenactment.

Contusions are evident in such cases as domestic violence, sexual battery, or child abuse. Contusions do not always have to be associated with a death investigation, although the previously stated violent acts can lead to a murder investigation. If the death is delayed, it can be attributed to the previously named violent acts. It is precisely for this reason that contusions such as handprints (as if the victim were spanked or slapped), finger patterns (like the victim was grabbed and held), linear patterns (common with belts or whips), and tread marks (run over by a vehicle) need to be documented. These contusions are associated with everything from child abuse, sexual battery, and domestic violence, to traffic homicide. There are many other types of contusions and patterns that can be best discussed and observed during a medicolegal course or during an interview with a medical examiner.

An investigator has to be aware that there are many aspects of blunt force trauma which cannot be learned or studied in a short period. There is also the possibility that an investigator might have limited exposure with such injuries based on the area where they work. Some police departments may investigate less than five murder cases a year and other agencies, in cities such as Chicago or Baltimore, are investigating hundreds of cases. Experience and exposure to a multitude of incidents allow investigators to garner the knowledge and proficiency needed to become well rounded when investigating cases associated with Blunt Force Trauma.

In order for a homicide investigator or violent crime investigator to be successful, they must start with the approach taken during the initial crime-scene investigation. Investigating the crime scene of a violent crime, especially a homicide, must be carried out in a systematic and methodical manner. This part of the investigation is crucial especially when the victim has suffered from a *gunshot wound(s)*, and is either critical or deceased. Every piece of information obtained while investigating the crime scene is critical to how the investigation will proceed.

The information or evidence uncovered by the lead investigator must be disseminated to the medical examiner.

To keep gun violence in perspective, in the United States between 2010 and 2013, over 60% of homicide deaths were a result of gunshot injuries. In 2015, firearms were used to kill over 13,286 people, excluding suicide deaths. It was no mystery that in 2013, gun violence in the United States attributed for 73,505 non-fatal gunshot-wound injuries and 33,636 deaths directly related to firearms. Additionally, there were 11,208 homicides, 21,175 suicides, 505 accidental or negligent deaths, and 281 deaths caused by a firearm with 'undetermined intent.' In 2012, 8,855 homicides were directly attributed to violent confrontations with firearms. When looking at the numbers, there was a significant increase of 2353 victims dying from gunshot-wound injuries. When location was discussed in the Mental Preparation chapter, it eluded to the potential investigator that they needed to understand the dynamics of certain locations within the city that they work. This is important because when investigating violent crimes or homicides, most of the victims or offenders are young adult males or male juveniles. Furthermore, gun violence is most prevalent in poor urban areas and closely associated with gang violence in some form or another.

Investigators have an obligation to understand the basic principles of gunshot wounds and how to interpret them. Gunshot wounds are physical traumas caused from a discharged firearm or munitions. Firearms cause most gunshot wounds that an investigator will encounter, like during a criminal confrontation, self-inflicted (intentional), accidental event, or military action (if you were in combat). The lead investigator along with the medical examiner need to collaborate throughout this type of investigation. To the investigator, it may be apparent that the victim sustained a gunshot wound(s), but additional information needs to be gathered so that the medical examiner can determine manner of death. As previously noted, if evidence is not properly documented, processed, and collected at the scene, once the victim and any possible evidence has been removed from a crime scene, any possible evidence remaining can be lost.

The lead investigator's responsibility, while on a crime scene, is to communicate with the crime-scene technician on what best practice can be used to properly preserve evidence or trace evidence. Concerning a victim of a gunshot wound, valuable evidence can be lost when the body is moved or mishandled. Conversely, extraneous evidence can be introduced that otherwise should not be part of the crime scene. For obvious reasons, a victim(s) body should be handled as little as possible so that valuable evidence is not moved or lost. Trace evidence that has transferred to a victim(s) clothing needs to be preserved and collected in an environment conducive for such a task. It is important for the victim, while on the scene, to be handled minimally. Under best practices, the victim should be placed onto a sterile, plastic sheet before being examined. This procedure will prevent trace evidence from being lost or non-evidentiary evidence from being introduced. An investigator must know, hands and fingers should not be touched or opened before being processed. Items such as hair, fibers, or other substances can be lost. An investigator cannot allow the victim to be contaminated prior to being processed and examined.

It is important to always conduct the physical examination of the victim with gloves; this limits the possibility (in theory) of transferring gunshot residue from the investigator to the victim. Once the on-scene physical examination has been completed by the medical examiner, make sure that the crime-scene technician places paper bags over the victim's hands to avoid losing any evidence. The victim's hands can be examined closely upon arrival at the morgue, prior to the postmortem. Then, the evidence can be documented and collected. So, as a lead investigator, one must remember to bag the victim's hands with a paper bag and not a plastic bag, because plastic bags can create condensation and that can cause evidence to be washed away. There will be occasions when the victim(s) will be transported to the morgue while inside a vehicle, if that is where the terminal event took place. For those moments, the vehicle is placed on a flatbed tow truck, secured. The victim(s) is covered with a sterile blanket to avoid being viewed by the public. Once the tow truck arrives at the morgue, the vehicle with the victim inside is rolled off the flatbed and placed in a secured garage bay. Once inside the morgue's bay, the lead investigator and the on-call state attorney will determine if a search warrant will be needed (this will be covered in the State Attorney chapter) for the victim's vehicle. If not, the procedure for the physical examination is different. The victim is removed from inside the vehicle and placed in one of the morgue's trays that has been lined with a sterile, plastic sheet. This allows for any evidence, if moved, to fall onto the sheet.

Basic knowledge of *firearms* is crucial during the course of investigating an incident where the victim was shot, it is important for the investigator assigned as the lead on the case to interpret the gunshot-wound injuries. Investigators, at some point during the course of the trial phase, may have to testify as to types of weapons or bullets, projectiles, casings, and fragments. Having common knowledge of such items or evidence does not mean that they are experts. It just acknowledges that they have an understanding of the terminology with respects to firearms. The investigator must know the difference between a semiautomatic and a revolver.

Such as, the *revolver* holds ammunition inside a cylinder, in individual chambers. In addition, the cylinder rotates, causing the chamber housing the bullet to align with the barrel. At this point, when the trigger is squeezed, the hammer drops and causes an explosion, which launches the bullet through the barrel. There can also be a double-action revolver that when the trigger is squeezed, the projectile is propelled, the hammer then stays in the cocked position waiting for the next trigger squeeze. Once the revolver has fired all rounds, the chambers must be emptied by hand. The explosion of the hammer striking the primer causes gases and powder to escape through the gaps between the cylinder and barrel. These gases and powders can result in the shooter to have gunshot residue (G.S.R.) on the hand and sometimes clothes. Individuals in close proximity to the shooter can also obtain G.S.R. particles, even if they did not fire the weapon.

Another firearm commonly used in violent crimes is the *semiautomatic* handgun. Understanding such a weapon is crucial to the investigator investigating an incident where the victim sustained a gunshot wound or multiple gunshot wounds. Casings discovered at a crime scene must be documented as to where they were found, in proximity to the decedent. These casings will give the investigative team clues as to what type of weapon was used. Locating, documenting, and recovering such evidence as casings, projectiles, and fragments is crucial to the investigation. These pieces of evidence are available because of the unique way in which the semiautomatic handgun functions.

Semiautomatic pistols do not have a cylinder and are auto-loading. In auto-loading, the trigger must be squeezed each time the weapon is fired. The force generated by the fired round allows the weapons mechanism (slide) to *extract and eject the spent casing* while simultaneously loading a fresh round into the chamber. An important part of the semiautomatic weapon is the magazine or 'clip.' Any number of magazines house different amounts of rounds, from one to sixteen (normal capacity) and there are extended magazines that can house over twenty rounds (not common). When discussing rifles, there are some magazines that can house up to one-hundred rounds (drum configuration). Investigators should keep in mind that magazines house rounds in various ways, single stack, alternate (side by side), or a cylindrical manner (drum form).

Once the magazine has been filled, it is then inserted into the grip portion of the semiautomatic pistol. The semiautomatic is then charged by manually pulling the slide back. This function allows for the top round in the magazine to enter the pistol's chamber. At this point, the semiautomatic pistol is charged and ready to be fired. Remember, once the trigger is squeezed, the round is fired and the casing is ejected. In over 95% of the cases, the casing is ejected to the right of the pistol.

Upon coming in contact with a semiautomatic pistol that has been located in a crime scene, the investigator must document if the slide of the pistol was fully to the rear of the pistol or partially to the rear. This will tell the investigator if the pistol is empty or if a casing has not completely ejected. In either case, the manner in which the pistol was located must be documented before making the pistol safe to handle. Investigators must check to see if the magazine is still inserted or removed. If the magazine is still inserted, an investigator must consider the pistol to be hot (ready to fire again). At this point in the investigation, the pistol must be documented (photographed), then *made safe.* Safety is paramount when handling any weapon in a crime scene. Therefore, in order to make the weapon safe, a trained officer must be notified if there is nobody on the investigative team that can secure the pistol safely. There will be times when the crime-scene technician assigned to the case can safely secure the weapon. The lead investigator or whomever was assigned to investigate the crime scene must document how the weapon was found, who found it, if it was handled or moved prior to the investigative team arriving on scene, and who touched it. These are questions that the lead investigator must have answered if they are to properly brief the medical examiner assigned to the case.

Earlier, rifles were brought to light when semiautomatic pistols were discussed. *Rifles* or *long guns* have been used in many violent incidents that are investigated daily across the country. As reported on, all too often, most of the recent mass-casualty incidents involved some type of rifle or semiautomatic pistol. Some of these rifles were modified in some way or another in order to maximize firepower to purposefully inflict as much damage as possible. Rifles are high velocity weapons which most citizens believe are strictly for military use. The notion that these weapons are strictly for military use is incorrect, but that topic is for another type of discussion. For the purpose of violent crimes, investigators need to understand that high velocity weapons (rifles) cause devastating damage to hard surfaces (walls, vehicles, buildings, etc.) as well as the human body. Various types of rifles, such as *Bolt-Action* (commonly used for hunting large game) uses a bolt which manually slides to the rear and chambers a round and once fired, the shooter must pull the bolt to the rear in order to eject the spent casing and repeat the initial process in order to chamber another round. This type of weapon can be hand feed (one round at a time into the chamber) or uses a three to five round magazine that fits under the weapon. However, the shooter must still pull the bolt to the rear in order to chamber another round.

The *Shotgun* is another type of long rifle and again, mostly used for hunting fowl or skeet shooting. There are various types of shotgun sold, such as single barrel, double barrel, pump-action, lever-action, or auto-loading. The barrels of these rifles are smooth bore and leave no grooves. Rounds for shotguns vary; just know that these rounds can be anything from birdshot to slug rounds.

Semiautomatic rifles such as the *AR-15, AK-47,* or *308 SASS* are rifles that are commonly used in violent acts. There are many brands, makes, and models which can be modified for a specific reason or function. Many of these weapons fall into the wrong hands and are used to commit the most heinous of crimes. These rifles, like the semiautomatic pistol, employee the same method of loading, charging, firing the round, and ejecting the casing. The big difference between the rifle and the pistol or revolver is the distance and velocity of the round that is fired. A rifle is meant to be more accurate at a greater distance and being a high velocity weapon, the damage that it can cause is tremendous, because energy increases with velocity.

Investigators need to understand that handguns and rifles have specific signatures, individual to each weapon. This is what sets the weapons apart from each other and enables the experts in the field of weapons and ballistics to compare casings or projectiles and match them to a specific weapon. Once a weapon is identified through scientific means, this enables the investigator to chart a course that may lead to the offender. The results of the ballistic testing are recorded into the National Integrated Ballistics Information Network (N.I.B.I.N.) database, if a link is made with another piece of evidence. The results are then prepared in a report and sent to the lead investigator. This report matches casings found at a crime scene to a particular weapon that might have been used at another incident. When a rifle or semiautomatic weapon is tested in the lab, it is fired in an environment where the projectile and casing can be retrieved and examined. The firing of the weapon causes what is known as 'rifling,' which is the spinning motion of the bullet as it travels through the barrel until it exits. The rifling creates what are known as 'Lands & Grooves,' these markings transfer to the bullet or jacket when fired. That is why it is so important to locate a bullet with minimal damage for future analysis by a *ballistics expert.*

There are many types of handguns and rifles, each have their own characteristics. These characteristics allow ballistics experts to identify weapons used in violent crimes or other crimes by markings or signatures left on located and documented evidence (bullets). An investigator must have an understanding of the terminology used when discussing firearms. The information learned during this section is to assist the new investigator or young attorney to communicate better with the experts in the field of firearms or ballistics. This section will not make an investigator an expert in firearms or ballistics, but will give them a working knowledge of how to approach a crime scene involving a victim who has sustained some sort of gunshot wound(s). It will assist the lead investigator in presenting the findings at the crime scene to the medical examiner.

A majority of the violent crimes and homicide cases investigated were a result of the victim being shot in some form or another. Investigating violent crimes or homicides are difficult and they each present unique characteristics that can make a simple investigation turn south quickly. But as previously noted, *all investigations*, no matter how simple they look or how difficult, starts at the crime scene.

Gunshot-wound deaths come in different forms, such as homicide, suicide, accidental, or undetermined (rare classification). The reasons for why these deaths occurred vary from case to case and circumstances; from a violent encounter, robbery gone wrong, and unfamiliarity with a weapon, to mental illness. It is important for the lead investigator to communicate with the medical examiner as to what precipitated the terminal event. During the on-scene briefing that is held by the lead investigator in order to pass out vital information that has been learned to the on-scene physical examination of the victim, the investigator should have established how many rounds were fired and how many might have struck the victim. At the onset, the exact number of gunshot wounds sustained by the victim will be undetermined until the on-scene physical examination (possibly). The accurate number of gunshot wounds will be determined at the postmortem. The investigator should be able to inform the medical examiner if a weapon was located at the crime scene and if the victim(s)'s hands were examined for any foreign objects or defects.

The investigator, along with the crime-scene technician, needs to determine the distance (as close as possible) from where the victim was shot in relationship to the casings (unless a revolver was used) that were located at the crime scene. Distance is a great indicator to the investigator and the medical examiner in order to discount suicide, unless the gunshot wound was close range. Self-inflicted gunshot wounds must be closely examined to eliminate an area that the victim could not reach unless via a self-made device. The investigative team must be cognizant of the crime scene and answer questions that can clear any doubt surrounding the incident. All questions can be answered by examining the physical evidence on the scene, the information learned while interviewing witnesses, and during the collection of additional evidence. The lead investigator must provide the medical examiner with the information that was collected during the initial investigation. The medical examiner must have this or any additional information prior to the postmortem being performed on the victim. The information given to the medical examiner, along with the findings of the postmortem, will assist the medical examiner in ruling on the cause and manner of death.

Gunshot-wound injuries vary due to the disruption of human tissues. Velocity of the bullet plays an important role with the amount of damage caused on the victim. An investigator can attempt to interpret the velocity of the projectile by using the formula referring to *Kinetic Energy* (KE=1/2 MV2 (M=Mass and V=Velocity)). The lead investigator will examine the victim's wounds with the medical examiner during the on-scene physical examination of the victim. As the victim is being examined, the investigator, along with the medical examiner, can hypothesize as to what area of the body was affected. Something that an investigator should be aware of if a victim has been transported to the nearest trauma center, is that immediate effects caused by a gunshot wound is typically severe loss of blood and potential shock to vital organs from oxygenated blood not being delivered. In the event that a victim is being treated in the trauma unit, an investigator should speak with the trauma physician in order to ascertain where the victim sustained their wounds. Areas of great concern would be if the victim sustained gunshot wounds to the chest (lungs/heart), lower torso (liver/kidneys) or genitals. Devastating gunshot wounds can also occur to a victim's head (brain) or spinal cord. Such wounds, which damage the central nervous system, are often fatal. Clearly, 95% of victims who sustain gunshot wounds to the head that affects the brain do not survive. The 5% that do survive have a long recovery depending on how the projectile entered the brain and which hemisphere was damaged and to what extent.

During this examination, whether in the field or at the trauma center, any evidence of value will be documented, processed, and collected. All wounds will be documented, but the exact number of wounds will not be known until the postmortem is performed. If an exact number of gunshot wounds cannot be determined during the on-scene physical examination, I use terms such as multiple or undetermined to complete the medical examiner report and the major's memorandum. Investigators must take into account lighting conditions, climate, location, and if the victim(s) clothing were removed or kept on. These factors play a big role and guessing is not an accepted practice by any investigator or the medical examiner.

What are *classic entrance wounds?* In order to understand what these wounds are like, an investigator, when observing a victim that has sustained wounds, must recognize the environment in which the victim was located and the lighting condition of the crime scene. A majority of entrance wounds may appear to look alike from a distance or to the untrained eye, but they are not. Entrance wounds have round or oval-type shapes and with an edge of chafed skin. These areas of abrasion are a result of the bullet scraping the edges of the skin as it enters the body. *Symmetrical wounds* are caused when the bullet enters the body at a right angle. If the wound appears to be *asymmetrical,* that indicates that the bullet entered at an angle. If the elasticity around a wound is released and there appears to be an attempt for the edges of the wound to re-approximate, this will create a central defect or a hole in the skin. Usually, the skin of an exit wound tends to re-approximate. An investigator cannot begin to guess what caliber of weapon was used based on the size of the wound. Since a body has areas where the skin may be tauter or wobbly, these characteristics do not allow for an accurate estimate of the bullet size. Therefore, an investigator must depend on the physical evidence located and recovered in the crime scene along with what is recovered from the body cavity during the postmortem.

Various types of gunshot wounds will be observed by investigators throughout their career. The following are some of these wounds, such as *ricochet-entrance wounds*; this type of wound can be caused by projectiles that have been deformed or fragmented after ricocheting. A victim may sustain one or multiple entrance wounds from the ricochet and these wounds can be superficial or irregular. The cause of these wounds is difficult to determine unless physical evidence is found at the crime scene. Evidence can be marks on a wall or pavement. If projectiles or fragments are located, they should be documented and collected. It is important for the investigator to brief the medical examiner on these findings.

Investigators will be confronted with *atypical entrance wounds.* The medical examiner assigned to the investigation will discuss this type of wounds. This type of wounds has a variation in the contour of the surface of the body such as the nose, lips, and ears. In addition, different skin texture (hands, eyelids, and scrotum) can give wounds an irregular appearance. High velocity weapons or unusual ammunition can cause atypical entrance wounds. These type-entrance wounds are best discussed with the medical examiner during the postmortem examination.

Shored wounds can be both entrance and exit, and are distinct by the abraded edges. The abrasions formed are broader and irregular than a typical entrance wound. However, as the bullet exits, it causes the skin to turn outward, which may rub against a foreign object, creating a shoring effect on the exit wound. An article of clothing (caps, belts, etc.) or the ground can cause this type of supported shored wound. This is because the bullet enters through an article of clothing which is in direct contact with the skin. This affects the skin surface, causing shoring. A common wound that an investigator will observe is a wound that enters a part of the body like the chest, exits the chest, and enters the arm. This is noted as a reentrance wound. Re-entrance wounds are best defined during the postmortem when the color rods (used to demonstrate wound path) are inserted into the wounds. This enables the medical examiner and the investigator to observe the direction of the projectiles travel.

Graze wounds or *defects* are gunshot wounds that skim across the skin of the body. Characteristics of a graze wound is an elongated abrasion which can be superficial or deep. There is another type of wound, *tangential,* which extends through the skin entering the subcutaneous (dermal) tissue and there are cases where tears are observed along the edges of the wound. These types of wounds are triangular in shape with apices that allows the investigator to determine from which direction the bullet came.

There will be incidents where the victim(s) is shot through objects such as car doors, windows, or a wooden door. In these cases, the victim sustains wounds that are altered because of the bullet's trajectory through a specific object. The object that is struck first is referred to as an *intermediary target.* The intermediary target may cause the bullet to break into fragments or secondary projectiles. Additionally, there may be parts of the intermediate target that can splinter or break, and these pieces may break the skin and, in some cases, might enter the body. Difficulties resulting from intermediate target wounds are that distance can be difficult to determine because it eliminates stippling, soot, or any gunshot residue (G.S.R.). In some suicide cases or homicides where a pillow is used, the victim did not have evidence such as gunpowder residue, stippling, or soot on the body because the pillow filtered this evidence. In cases such as these, the documentation and processing of the crime scene is crucial. The information gathered must be provided to the medical examiner by the investigator. All evidence must be collected so that the medical examiner can carefully inspect the item(s) in question.

During the course of the on-scene physical examination or during the postmortem of the victim, the *exit wound* will be inspected. Investigators need to know that *exit wounds* are tears or lacerations at the point where the projectile exited the victim's body. The exit wounds' characteristics are generally the same, independent of the distance from where the victim(s) is shot. These gunshot wounds range from irregular, linear, crescent, or stellate-shaped. Stellate wounds may be confused with hard contact wounds, especially on the head. Some stellate wounds may be larger than entrance wounds. Additionally, these wounds have no rim abrasions and the edges re-approximate. There will be instances when a projectile enters soft tissue, but does not have enough force to exit the body, on these occasions, the projectile might be partially protruding under the skin where it is visible and sometimes, the projectile is partially through the skin, but does not completely exit the body. Some of these gunshot wounds may be a result of the victim being in a supported position.

Investigators should be able to evaluate gunshot wounds and determine (not exactly) the *range of fire.* An investigator, along with the crime-scene technician, should be able to evaluate from the different types of entrance wounds the range of fire. Keep in mind that gunshot wounds vary from close contact, intermediate, to an undetermined distance (unspecified). This is an important reason for knowing basic terminology that will assist the investigator when communicating with professionals in specific fields, as well as the medical examiner. Some of the basic terms used previously in this section are; gas (seen in contact wounds), soot (complete combustion of gunpowder), and primer compounds such as copper/nickel that vaporizes from a cartridge case or metal that vaporizes from a bullet/jacket, flame at 1400 F and bullet.

An investigator is not supposed to be an expert in every facet of weapons or gunshot wounds, but they must have a general/advanced understanding in order to proficiently and thoroughly investigate a violent crime. An investigator must know that *fouling* is soot or residue of completely burned powder; it is dust-like and can be wiped off. *Stippling or tattooing* is burned or unburned powder and debris which causes punctuated impressions on the victim's skin and do not wipe off. This is heavier than soot and larger, thus it travels further. Something to keep in mind, *'stippling' is not a 'powder burn'*, it is not a burn at all; it is an abrasion/defect which is caused by the particles striking the victim's skin. When a projectile travel through a victim's clothing, it leaves a ring of gray or black discoloration from dirt and lubricant that comes from the barrel of the gun used. The dirt and lubricant are rubbed off when it passes through a victim's clothing or skin. This evidence is known as *'bullet wipe.'* A good indicator that differentiates 'soot' from 'bullet wipe'; soot is dark in color or black in the center, and it begins to lighten as it moves away from the center of the gunshot wound, as opposed to 'bullet wipe' which is consistent and generally is seen on one side of the entrance hole or edge without involving surrounding fabric. Knowing each of the above aspects enables the investigator to communicate with the investigative team and the medical examiner.

As stated in the previous sections, there are various types of gunshot wounds and each have distinct characteristics, depending on the weapon used, distance, and intermediate obstacles that the projectile strikes prior to making contact with the victim. *Contact wounds* are caused when the barrel/muzzle of a gun makes contact with the victim's skin. In cases when the barrel of the gun is held tightly to the victim's skin (such as a suicide), it leaves an impression known as a 'muzzle stamp,' a patterned abrasion can be observed at the entrance wound which is caused by contact. In these types of wounds, investigators should understand that gun smoke enters the wound, but small amounts of it might be seen around the edges of the wound, especially if it was a loose contact wound. In such case, there may be a small ring of soot on the skin surrounding the entrance wound without noticeable stippling. In cases where the wound is dry and black, tissue will be removed from this section so that specialists can examine it closely for any presence of gunpowder residue. An investigator should be looking for 'blow back,' this occurs when soft-tissue evidence (blood, tissue, brain matter, hair, etc.) is observed inside the barrel of the gun from the exploding gases when the gun is fired. Investigators, along with the crime-scene technician, should attempt to examine the gun used at the crime scene for any tissue around the barrel/muzzle or distal end. Clothing was illustrated in the previous section; therefore, it is important to examine clothing worn by the victim when the shooting took place, which might have been a barrier between the barrel and skin. *Blow-back* evidence is most common in head wounds. These wounds are caused by the barrel/muzzle of the gun pressed tightly against a victim's head/skull and as the gun is fired, the exploding gases disrupt the pocket between the skin and bone. Stellate wounds (discussed earlier) are common due to tears that emit from the sides of the wound. An investigator will observe overstretching of the skin that is caused by epidermal tears from the trapped gases. An investigator must not confuse these types of wounds as exit wounds.

Now that an investigator has a general understanding of contact wounds, additional wounds such as close range, intermediate, and distant wounds will be described. *Close range* wounds can be described as gunshot wounds where the barrel does not touch the victim's skin. Usually, the distance is six inches or less, with stippling as well as fouling being present around the wound. Investigators must understand that soot surrounding the wound will increase in area and the density of soot deposits will lessen as the barrel moves away from the victim. It is important to know that soot vanishes beyond one foot of firing a gun. Intermediate wounds have stippling but fouling is not present. *Intermediate* wounds are caused from distances of less than an inch to thirty inches, and as the firing distance increases, there is a wider and less-dense pattern of stippling. Now, *distance* wounds have no fouling or stippling, and the distance from the victim is greater than thirty inches. There might be cases when stippling and fouling are not present, but that does not mean a gun was fired from a distance. The lack of stippling and fouling in some cases can be attributed to clothing, intermediary objects, hair, or other factors.

When investigating a homicide scene, the investigator, through powers of observation and if possible, with witness accounts, can attempt to discern what is before them, when viewing a victim that has multiple gunshot wounds. There is a possibility that the victim was shot multiple times, but what if the victim sustained a gunshot wound from a shotgun. *Shotgun* wounds have characteristics such as a single wound or multiple wounds (caused by pellets or *00 Buck* shot). People normally equate a shotgun wound as being dynamic and with many individual wounds entering the body. What people do not understand and investigators must look for, is the single dynamic wound caused by a *slug round.* A wound caused by this type of round has a devastating effect on the body. If a victim is shot at close range with a shotgun round filled with pellets, there is a possibility that a single wound is observed because the pellets do not have room to spread. However, if the victim is shot from a distance, multiple wounds will be observed, especially with a round filled with pellets. As the distance increases, the pattern presented by the pellets can vary. Another piece of evidence that must be considered, was the victim struck with the wadding material from the shotgun. Normally, as the shotgun round is fired and the pellets are expelled, the plastic wadding follows through the barrel and falls to the ground. Except, if the shotgun was fired within three feet, the wading may strike the body, leaving a circular mark. Investigators need to understand when working shotgun incidents, that circular cardboard wadding can leave abrasions and patterns from approximately fifteen feet and twenty feet if the wadding was plastic. Now, a shotgun wad can enter a body up to 10 feet away and can travel much further. As previously stated, if the shotgun wound is singular, there is the possibility that the wad entered the body. (However, if there are multiple shotgun wounds in the body, the possibility of finding the wadding inside the body is nonexistent. It is important for the investigative team to meticulously search the death scene where a shotgun was used. It is especially important if the victim sustained multiple wounds.)

During the course of investigating the crime scene, communication between the lead investigator, his team, the crime-scene technician, and the medical examiner is paramount in order to achieve positive results when investigating violent incidents, especially death cases that are caused by gunshots. As a rule, I advise all my new investigators to treat each case as if it were a homicide. This ensures that the investigator will be extra careful and not overconfident. Deaths that occur from gunshots can be anything from homicide, suicide, accidental, and in some cases, undetermined. For this reason, as stated in the crime-scene section, the on-scene investigation by the lead investigator and crime-scene technician must be performed methodically, documented, and processed thoroughly. Many variables come into play in cases where the victim has died from a gunshot wound or multiple gunshot wounds. Where was the gunshot wound or the distance as it relates to the wound? If a gunshot wound is located in an area of the body that is not accessible by the victim, homicide must be considered as a motive. In cases where the gunshot wound is in the mouth, temple, and forehead, suicide is most likely. In order for the medical examiner to properly classify the incident being investigated, the information learned during the crime-scene investigation, along with witness accounts, is paramount and must be a part of the briefing with the medical examiner.

There will be instances when a violent-crimes team responds to an incident where a victim or victims are being treated for gunshot-wound injuries. The lead investigator in such cases must evaluate the victims upon arrival on the crime scene and determine if any of the victims may be suffering from potential life-threatening injuries. This information can be obtained from the fire-rescue personnel who are treating the victims at the scene prior to transporting them to the nearest emergency/trauma facility. Once the investigator determines that a victim has a likelihood of not surviving their injuries, the on-call homicide team must be put on notice. Once a homicide team has been made aware of the victim's condition, a team member will probably shadow the violent-crimes team until such time that the victim is pronounced deceased.

Once a victim is transported to the emergency/trauma facility, an investigator on the investigating team (violent crimes or homicide) must respond to the hospital in order to evaluate the progress of the trauma team and to speak with the lead-trauma physician in order to gather information regarding the victim's condition. If the victim was brought to the emergency/trauma facility clothed, what was done with the clothing? The victim's clothing is evidence which needs to be processed and collected by the crime-scene technician or sent to the medical examiner's office with the victim. Even though life-saving measures will be immortalized in the hospital notes (these notes will be given to the medical examiner by the hospital), the investigator that responds to the hospital should ask if surgery was required and if so, was a projectile or projectiles removed from the victim during the surgery. If they were, they are placed into what investigators refer to as a 'bullet box.' The crime-scene technician assigned to the investigation will collect evidence from the 'bullet box' and send the evidence to the lab in order for it to be examined.

Depending on the life-saving measures taken by the trauma staff, a victim may be kept alive for several days, weeks, months, and even years, if they are sent to a convalescent facility. There have been cases where a victim of a gunshot wound has died several years later. These delayed deaths are then reclassified from aggravated battery/attempted murder, to murder.

In the event that a victim dies well after the initial incident took place *(delayed death)* from complications as a result of their injuries, it is important to review all of the original reports and supplements pertaining to the case. For this reason, the initial response by the homicide investigator was so important. All relevant information needs to be reviewed by the new investigator and their team in order to get a new perspective surrounding the incident. Although the homicide investigator did not participate with the original investigation, they should have kept abreast of the incident by communicating with the violent-crimes investigator and hope that the original investigator investigated the incident to the fullest. This would make the transition from an aggravated battery/attempted murder investigation to a murder investigation much easier. I hope that major crimes units work cooperatively and their egos put aside for the betterment of the case and justice for the victim. After a thorough review of all documents and reports pertaining to a delayed death, the lead investigator must brief the medical examiner of the circumstances regarding the terminal event.

In closing this section, the investigator should have a better perspective of gunshot wounds and the damage they are capable of inflicting. Additionally, investigators need to recognize what a gunshot-wound injury looks like and how many gunshot wounds a victim has sustained. If a victim is wounded by a shotgun, rifle, or handgun, what characteristics do the wounds have? Investigators are trained to document what they observe and what is learned from interviewing witnesses, these facts are true. What an investigator cannot do is tailor facts to fit the crime because at the end of the investigation, physical evidence does not lie. The proper supervision of how evidence is documented, processed, and collected is pertinent to the investigation and to the medical examiner. For this reason, continuous communication between the investigator and the medical examiner is so vital in determining how the victim died and what the ruling would be.

Stabbing Injuries

In the previous chapters, emphasis was placed on crime-scene preservation and how to process a crime scene to avoid losing valuable evidence. Additionally, the lead investigators' responsibility to avoid contaminating a crime scene through carelessness is crucial. This is especially true when investigating a violent incident involving *sharp force injuries,* such as *stabbings* or *cutting.* Incidents where victims were severely cut or stabbed are not as rare as some might think. In the United States, stabbing deaths are four times higher than deaths from a person shot by a rifle. Crime scenes of stabbings or severe cuts tend to appear more gruesome than gunshot incidents. The personal nature of stabbing incidents makes investigating such cases easier. A stabbing or cutting incident, in most cases, is closely associated with a passionate encounter, not one where distance creates the personal buffer.

An investigator should have a clear understanding of how to interpret injuries caused by sharp force and be able to properly communicate with team members, crime-scene technicians, and the medical examiner using the proper terminology. Documentation and the processing of the crime scene is crucial in being able to interpret injuries caused by stabbing or cutting. The way in which the force causes the injury will determine how the injuries are classified. As previously stated, in the United States, death caused by stabbings are four times greater than deaths caused by rifles.

Instruments that are used to inflict great bodily injury, whether lethal or non-lethal, leave wounds with distinctive markings (tool marks). These wounds/injuries leave patterns on the skin and in the soft tissues. These sharp force injuries are caused by instruments with sharp edges, as opposed to blunt force injuries, which are caused by a weapon with a flat or smooth surface, such as bat, hammer, floor, or inside of a car (steering wheel). Knives cause the majority of fatal sharp force injuries, but other type of sharp instruments like box-cutter, glass, or any object with a sharp edge have the ability to inflict the same fatal injury. When investigators exam a crime scene and the victim (whether deceased or not), they should document what types of wounds were discovered. Injuries can be from a stab or a cut (incised wound). The investigator, when documenting each wound, should determine what the wound's category is. If the wound is from a stabbing, it is reflected as deep. Conversely, if the wound is longer than deep, then it is most likely a cut or incised wound.

Other types of forced trauma can be caused from instruments/weapons such as hatchet, machete, claw hammer, or an axe. The injuries caused by these weapons tend to be choppier and some are derived from a sharp and crushing blow to the victim. Some of these injuries are distinguished by the characteristics of the wound and the force used to inflict the injury. Sharp force wounds are different from lacerations because of tissue that is torn due to blunt force. With lacerated wounds, the investigator should look for irregular, abraded margins and bridging of tissue. As the physical examination of the victim is conducted, an investigator can conclude, when documenting the injuries with the medical examiner, that such injuries were created by blunt force because the lacerations are irregular, jagged, and have abraded margins. Whereas, if the injuries are caused by stabbing, then the physical examination will reveal that the energy used the cause such injuries were distributed over a small area and the wounds are usually straight and non-abraded.

During the course of discussing certain types of wounds associated with sharp force injuries, the medical examiner may refer to an injury as *bridging.* Investigators need to know that *bridging* or *tissue bridging* speaks to strands of tissue that extend from one edge of a wound to the other side of the wound. In knife wounds, when the knife penetrates the skin, the blade instantly severs all of the tissues between the edges of the wound. Conversely, when a blunt object causes the injury, the weapon does not interpolate itself between the edges of the tear in the tissue. In this instance, the force of the object causes the tissue to stretch over the surface, causing the skin to tear.

When examining the victim, the investigator should document their observations as to where the injuries were located. This will greatly assist in discerning the type of wounds being examined. Lacerations, unlike incised wounds which can occur anywhere on the body, tend to be most prevalent around the eyebrows, scalp, elbows, and forehead.

Interestingly enough, not all wound characteristics can be relied upon to suggest blunt or sharp force injury. There are instances where tissue bridging or abraded margins are not identified in a laceration injury. Instead, a combination of blunt and sharp force can create a particular characteristic of a wound. It is at this point that the investigator must consult with the medical examiner to properly diagnose the wound and its cause. There are many variables which might disguise how an injury was caused, such as a dull-edged weapon, or a hatchet can create an injury that is both blunt and sharp force in nature. In observing these types of injuries, the investigator needs to be clear and understand that distinguishing between blunt force and sharp force injuries may not always be clear-cut.

Investigators should have enough knowledge of wounds to identify characteristics associated with a specific injury. During the preliminary stages of an investigation, when the lead investigator is examining the victim's injuries in the trauma unit (if alive) or at the scene (if deceased), the severity of the injury or injuries can establish from the force used or the motion of the weapon. When an investigator cannot do is attempt to say with certainty the type of weapon used based on the characteristics of the injury, knowing the type of weapon would be highly unlikely in the early stages of an investigation. This is another reason why canvassing the crime scene and interviewing witnesses or the victim (if alive) is critical, it can shed light as to how the incident took place and what weapon might have been used. If a weapon is recovered during the search of the crime scene, tool markings associated with that weapon can be closely examined during the postmortem. The results of the physical examination of the victim will assist with the investigation and to determine if a particular weapon was used.

While observing and assisting the medical examiner with the on-scene physical examination of the victim, it is the responsibility of the investigator to document where the wounds were located. The investigator must *keep in mind that not all wounds may be observed* during this examination. A detailed account and location of the wounds will be determined during the physical examination at the morgue. Investigators should compare how many wounds were documented at the crime scene as compared to the actual number of wounds documented during the postmortem. The difference and location of wounds will assist investigators in future investigation of similar incidents. The scene conditions and the condition of the victim plays a big part of how wounds are documented in sharp force and blunt force injuries. If the victim is in a state of decomposition, documenting the wounds would be very difficult while at the crime scene, just as if the victim was wearing heavy clothing, the victim's clothes would have to be removed at the crime scene in order to have a better idea of how many and where the wounds were located.

During the on-scene physical examination of the victim, the condition of the crime scene plays a huge role in how the examination will be performed or if the removal of the victim to a sterile environment would be better suited for the integrity of the investigation. The investigator, when documenting the injuries, should use plan language to describe location of the wounds and the type of injury. Anatomically, specific terms should be used when the investigator feels comfortable with the terminology, if not, keep it simple. Specific language to describe an injury or the location of the body such as posterior, anterior, or mid-lower back will be developed with experience. Additionally, a good relationship with the medical examiner goes a long way in understanding the verbiage used and the anatomical structure of the human body, though a good book on human anatomy can help.

The location of sharp force injuries can determine the *fatal factor*. If a victim sustained a wound to the neck, chest, or an area where vital organs or main arteries are located, the survival factor diminishes as opposed to sharp force or blunt force injuries to other areas of the body. Other areas of the body that need to be examined are hands, arms, and wrists. In a victim, these areas can be associated with *defensive wounds* or *suicide*. In the case of an offender, the hands are crucial because they can tell the investigator the kind of force that was used to commit the fatal act. In many cases, offenders will show cuts to the palms or the webbing areas between the thumb and index finger. *These injuries must be documented and photographed.* These wounds must be examined by the investigator and discussed with the medical examiner in order to determine the force used to create such a wound. Length and width of wounds are helpful, but they cannot determine the type of weapon used to produce the injury. This is true because the same weapon can create a long wound if it is used in a cutting manner. Additionally, the width of the wound can differ. If the victim is stabbed, depending on the location of the wound or the position of the victim, the force used can cause the wounds to gape or widen.

No investigator can determine how deep a stab wound is by merely looking at the injury. To properly document the depth of a wound, the investigator must attend the postmortem. Confer with the medical examiner and note the measurements taken of the wound at the time of the autopsy. The severity of the injury will determine the type of weapon and length of blade associated with the weapon used. Like any other sharp force injury, the depth of the injury will not always be precise; an investigator must know that some wounds may not be as deep as the weapon/blade used. During the postmortem, the investigator must maintain communication with the medical examiner in the event that additional information was learned concerning the type of weapon used or the size of the blade. It is important, if possible, to have the weapon (knife) present at the time of the postmortem, this will allow the medical examiner to closely examine it and make the proper comparisons. When there are multiple stab wounds, the possibility that each wound has dissimilar depths increases because of the nature of the incident. It would be highly unlikely that an offender, during the course of committing such an act, would be so deliberate and precise with the pressure to cause the injury.

Tool markings and the *signature* of a knife will assist the investigator and the medical examiner in determining the type of knife used during the course of the incident. Knives come in many shapes, sizes, and thickness. There are single-edged knives and double-edged knives. Single edged knives are ones that have the cutting edge on one side. Why would knowing this be important?

Investigators should understand that these two sets are referred to as *class* and *individual* characteristics. *Class characteristics* are caused from mass production which leaves distinct structural details on the tools surface. Cast molding, die stamping, or die forging can cause these markings. *Individual characteristics* are mainly caused by wear and tear of the tool/weapon. The ability to retain fine detail can decrease while retaining enough characteristics to allow for a positive identification of the weapon/tool. During the examination of the victim by the medical examiner, the investigator should pay close attention to detailed markings on bones. These cuts are specific to a particular type of weapon that has a distinct signature on the cutting edge. Tissue and cartilage, because their firm and soft texture will record finer detail, unlike bone. As the evolution of identifying weapons has evolved, today, scientists can establish individual characteristics or tool markings with a greater degree of certainty. W. Bonte (*Tool Marks in Bone and Cartilage,* Journal of Forensic Sciences, Vol. 20, No. Two, April, 1975) stated, "Saw marks and knife wounds in rib cartilage have yet to be mentioned in the Anglo-American literature." Yet, the German texts are replete with wounds of such nature.

Investigators must understand that it is very difficult to associate a single or double-edged wound to a specific weapon. A thin knife with a dull end cannot be differentiated on the skin. Something to consider is that a double-edged blade can cause a blunt end if the blade is slightly twisted in the body. In some injuries/wounds, depending on the depth of the wound, a knife with a double-edged tip and a single edge as it nears the handle can give the wound an appearance of a single or double-edged signature. **Note**: '*Ricasso*' is the unsharpened section adjacent to the knife handle. If the blade penetrates to the ricasso, it may possibly give the wound an appearance of two blunt ends.

Serrated injury patterns are most commonly produced with a knife that has a serrated edge, such as a common kitchen knife (steak knife). Such injury patterns consist of edges with jagged margins or abrasions that are closely spaced. These spaces should correlate to the spacing of the serrations on the blade. Obviously, once an investigator determines (after consulting with the medical examiner) that the injury pattern has characteristics of a serration, which gives strong indication, a serrated weapon was used to commit the injury. Investigators must know that not all blades have serrated edges. There are many different types of knives in the open market with distinct signatures and such signatures can leave specific tool-markings on a wound. There are far too many examples to mention, but utility knives is one that comes to mind. When the medical examiner refers to a wound having hilt marks, this refers to a knife that has been used with such penetrating force as to create contusions or abrasions on the skin, adjacent to the wound. This signature is caused from the hand guards reaching the skin during a dynamic penetration of the blade, thus leaving its mark. There are injuries where the knife did not penetrate deep enough and without enough force to produce a hilt mark. Investigators must keep in mind and understand that some wounds may or may not show evidence of a distinct characteristic. A wound caused by a serrated knife may leave serrated marks and there may be occasions where a serrated knife is used but no serrated evidence is distinguished. Therefore, absence of serrated signs cannot be the final determination of the weapon used. Additionally, it is important to note that during the course of stabbing the victim, the offender used such force that it caused the tip of a knife to break. This will be determined during the postmortem if the tip of the knife is located within the body cavity or even imbedded in a bone.

Another point to remember, in most cases, not all weapons can be identified from a wound-weapon comparison. However, residual bloodstains on a knife can be tested for D.N.A. comparison. A potential weapon cannot be brought within close proximity of a wound; this is to avoid contamination of a weapon that might not be the one that was used. An investigator must remember that a weapon comparison to the wound is quicker than a D.N.A. test.

Injuries that are caused from sharp force can be attributed to *chopping* wounds. Both sharp and crushing forces against the victim cause these wounds. Weapons that cause these types of wounds are normally heavier than other weapons, such as machetes, axes, propeller blades, machinery blades, or hatchets. Most chop-wounds extend to the underlying bone, which can cause the bone to fracture.

Defensive or Offensive Wounds

During the course of investigating a violent attack, the lead investigator must be able to discern the difference between defensive and non-defensive wounds. Non-defensive wounds can be interpreted as offensive wounds, which is why an investigator must be deliberate when examining the victim on the scene. The initial on-scene examination goes a long way in explaining what took place during the violent episode, whether the victim is alive or deceased, or during the course of the investigation, the investigator interviews a witness/offender with injuries consistent with offensive wounds. These are details that an investigator must relay to the medical examiner assigned to the case.

In over 20 years of investigating violent crimes, I have observed both defensive and offensive wounds associated with sharp force incidents. Much of these wounds can be difficult to decipher if the investigator is not meticulous during the course of the initial examination of victims or possible offenders. Another important factor is the initial interviews of witnesses and possible offenders. The results of these interviews can assist in piecing together how the violent event took place, who was an aggressor or victim.

Sharp force injuries that occur on the extremities of a victim during the course of a violent attack are commonly referred to as *defensive wounds.* These injuries take place when a victim attempts to fend off an attacker. Though defensive wound is a common term used in law enforcement and forensic texts, in New York, this term is avoided because of an appellate court ruling (People v Paschall, 91 A.D.2d 645) which stated that a jury and not an expert witness, should determine if such an injury was sustained while defending oneself (Gill and Catanese, 2002). These wounds are normally observed on the ventral surfaces of the hands which occurs when the victim attempts to grab a knife blade. Additionally, these injuries are typically observed on the dorsal surfaces of the forearms and hands. According to Gill and Catanese, defensive wounds are found in 49% of 101 sharp force homicides. Defensive wounds can also be seen in lower extremities of homicide victims where rape was a motivation during the attack. Also, according to Karlsson (1998a), defensive wounds were found in 41% of 174 sharp force homicides.

During the course of a violent attack, the offender may sustain *offensive wounds.* These wounds are caused when the knife handle slips (blade cuts across inner surface of the hand) through the offender(s) hands (palm and inside of the index finger or thumb) which creates the offensive wound. During the initial stages of the investigation, if the investigator is able to interview a possible offender, the hands should be examined and processed if such wounds are present. This information must be provided to the medical examiner. Another important factor that is crucial to the investigation pertains to the offender's blood possibly being present on the victim, especially in homicides where sharp force trauma is present. In examining the crime scene for blood-spatter patterns, the investigator, along with the crime-scene technician, must be careful not to disregard swabbing the blood. The offender might have transferred their blood onto the victim(s) clothes or an exposed body part. The crime-scene technician at the crime scene must collect the blood samples, or the samples can be collected prior to the postmortem. Again, referring to Karlsson (1998b), he noted that 27% of offenders had sharp force injuries to their hands when examined shortly after the violent event.

It has been my experience that during a violent episode where the victim(s) and offender(s) are closely related, injuries inflicted on the victim are overwhelming. These are passionate episodes where the offender(s) is fueled by extreme rage. Mental illness associated with the offender cannot be overlooked and is another factor that should be explored. In such cases, the offender uses sharp force to many parts of the victim's body, but mostly around the face or genitalia. During the processing of these crime scenes, it is suggested to use a rape kit to recover samples regardless of the victim's gender. These types of homicides are referred to as '*overkill.*' An exact number of wounds, excluding defensive wounds, has not been determined that will constitute an 'overkill.' Although, the general rule of thought is any number of wounds above 10.

Self-Inflicted or Hesitation Wounds...

Self-inflicted injuries caused by incised wounds are most common in suicides, most of the injuries associated with a suicide can be differentiated from those injuries inflicted during a homicide. Much of the evidence gathered during the initial investigation will lead an investigator toward the causation, such as the scene, terminal event, and the postmortem results. One important factor to consider, are the injuries in proximity to where the victim could have used their own hands? When referring to close proximity, one must consider injuries to the chest, neck, abdomen, arms, and wrists. Such self-mutilations should coincide with the results of the postmortem. If the wounds are to the back, an investigator can safely surmise that the victim had no part with mechanism of self-infliction. It is so important for the investigator to communicate with the medical examiner, because the findings during the postmortem will determine what the cause and manner of death will be. In such cases, the physical evidence should correlate with the terminal event when reviewing the timeline prior to the incident.

There are occasions when examining self-inflicted wounds, that additional minor (less lethal) injuries are observed. These minor injuries are known as *hesitation wounds.* These wounds are caused by preliminary or failed attempts to inflict a fatal injury. Such wounds can either be incised or stab wounds. These hesitation wounds can be superficial and multiple, usually they are parallel and adjacent to the fatal wound. I have always considered hesitation wounds as 'finding the courage' wounds because the victim makes multiple attempts until they finally achieve what they want (which is to die). An investigator must remember that there will be instances where hesitation wounds are not present. Additionally, hesitation marks can be observed when torture is inflicted prior to the terminal event. In such cases, the investigation should provide evidence that suggests suicide was not the cause and therefore, homicide would be the ruling. An investigator must keep in mind that though hesitation wounds are prevalent in suicides, the mere fact that they are present does not prove or suggest that the terminal event was suicide.

In 2002, a review by Gill and Catanese found that hesitation wounds were present in 65% of suicides. Additionally, Byard et al. (2002) found hesitation wounds in 54% of suicides. An investigator must consider, during the investigation, that the presence of multiple stab wounds should not rule out the classification of suicide. There may be instances where the victim self-inflicts multiple stab wounds with one of the wounds being fatal. Hesitation marks in close proximity also suggests that the victim was stationary and not attempting to fight off an attacker. In determining if the incident being investigated is a suicide, the investigator in conjunction with the medical examiner's final report of the postmortem, crime-scene report, and victim's medical history should be consistent with the death investigation's findings.

In summarizing this section, investigators should understand that injuries caused by sharp force represent distinguishing characteristics that separates them from injuries caused by blunt force. We have examined that sharp force injuries are commonly caused by knives, razors, or other sharp objects (not necessarily weapons). The investigator should know that characteristics associated with sharp force injuries such as hilt marks or serrations are closely associated with the weapon that was used to commit the injury (knife). Additionally, the investigator cannot become so confident as to overlook the fact that over-interpretation of a wound to identify a possible weapon is not always correct. Just like wounds that are absent of certain characteristics does not imply the absence of a specific weapon's characteristics. Remember that defensive wounds are wounds that are mostly observed on the hands, arms, occasionally in the lower extremities, which suggests that the victim tried to fight off the attacker. These are mostly incised wounds. In reference to self-inflicted sharp force injuries commonly observed in suicides, hesitation marks are classical features which are multiple, superficial, sharp force injuries parallel to the fatal wound. Other locations on the body where self-inflicted injuries are typically observed are abdomen, chest, neck, arms, and wrists. All of the information gathered by investigators during sharp force injury cases should correlate with the information gathered by the medical examiner during the postmortem. In reviewing the evidence, cause and manner of death can be determined.

Bibliography: J.R. Gill and C. Cantanese – 2002 Sharp Force injury fatalities in New York City, Journal of Forensic Sciences. R.W. Byrad – 2002 Clinical pathological features of fatal self-inflicted incised and stab wounds. American Journal of Forensic Medicine and Pathology. 23(1): 15-18.

Deaths Related to Sexual Assaults...

Having investigated few death cases where sexual assault was a component, led me to collaborate and assist special victims' investigators on their cases in order to get a better perspective of violent sexual assaults. During the course of investigating a homicide where the potential exist that a sexual event occurred whether forcefully or consensually, the crime scene and the way it gets documented always comes back to play an important part of the case. The collection of evidence at these crime scenes are paramount in order for them to be properly analyzed. It is vital for the investigator to inform the medical examiner of the potential that a sexual encounter took place prior to the terminal event. Investigators need to monitor how the crime-scene technician collected and preserved the evidence collected at the crime scene. As the investigator works closely with the medical examiner, they will have a better understanding of encountered *paraphilia*, patterned injuries, which will allow the medical examiner to determine causes and manners of death. The collaboration between the lead investigator and the medical examiner in death cases, which are a result of a sexual assault, is crucial. These cases are extremely difficult to investigate and, in most instances, multiple crime scenes are involved. For the investigator, familiarity with paraphilia will assist in determining if a sexual assault took place, also to better interpret the evidence that is documented and collected at the crime scene.

In my years of investigating death cases, most of those incidents that had a sexual component were mostly of an autoerotic or consensual in nature, where manual or ligature strangulation took place. In studies, it has been well documented that the most common causes of death in sexual assault cases are a result of asphyxia, blunt force trauma, and sharp force injuries. The victim(s) of cases where sharp force was a manner of death, the injuries were usually stabbing or incised wounds. Death from blunt force can be determined depending on how and where the injuries were inflicted. Many factors come into play in order to determine these patterns. In many of the death cases where blunt force or sharp force injuries were observed, 'overkill' is displayed. The 'overkill' is mostly due to rage, personal, and emotional conflict with the victim by the offender. Investigators are cautioned to be extremely careful with crime scenes when investigating death cases as a result of a sexual attack or no attack. Deaths from asphyxiation are mostly from manual strangulation, ligature strangulation, chest compression, or smothering (mouth and nose). Investigators might encounter cases where death was a result of a gunshot wound or other injuries that occurred during the sexual attack, but these are not common.

Manners of death in sexual assault cases are mainly homicide or suicide. *Homicide,* as defined, is the unwarranted, intentional death of a human being by another. The definition of homicide, during this section, is to assist the investigator, but it will be defined in depth later on in this book. *Suicide* is the intentional death of one's person by his or her own hands.

Investigators, when observing, documenting, and supervising the collection of evidence (suicide note) during an apparent suicide that is sexual in nature (which is rare), must understand that in order for the medical examiner to classify the manner of death as a suicide, there must be evidence to suggest a self-destructive nature. This information can be obtained when interviewing witnesses or recovering physical evidence such as a *suicide note* which details the intent and reason, or a history of previous suicide attempts. However, for the most part, death from sexual assaults are homicide related. As previously stated, autoerotic asphyxia or consensual sexual activity can result in death.

These deaths are usually classified as *accidental* by the medical examiner after reviewing the findings of the investigation. These rare cases are not classified as death by sexual assault.

Earlier in this section, *Paraphilia* was mentioned as being associated with deaths as a result of a sexual assault. So, what is paraphilia? Paraphilias are psychiatric sexual disorders or disorders of attraction (fatal attraction). This area is more geared toward the medical examiner, but the investigator should understand aspects which pertains to this disorder. According to the *Diagnostic and Statistical Manual of Mental Disorders*, fourth edition, published by the American Psychiatric Association (1996), it went on to recognize nine paraphilias and list their diagnostic criteria. These are just guidelines and not meant to categorize or classify offenders. Presently, this system only exists to classify and can be used with discretion. Therefore, investigators should maintain an open dialogue with the medical examiner concerning how cases will be classified. All paraphilias involve components of fantasy, sexual urge, and blatant behavior. Some of these paraphilias are; *Exhibitionism* (exposure of one's genitals to another), *Fetishism* (being involved sexually with inanimate objects), *Pedophilia* (having sexual encounter with a minor child of either sex), *Masochism* (sexual acts involving bondage or battery) and *Sadism* (sexual acts of physical or psychological anguish of someone else). These are but a few of the commonly used terms referred to paraphilias. There are many more and as an investigator, one should become familiar with each. Attending medicolegal courses or any training in the field of sexual deviant behavior is recommended throughout one's career because it is not always guaranteed that an investigator may be involved with such a case. Understanding paraphilias will assist the investigator in interpreting evidence that is located in a crime scene or why humiliating evidence on a victim occurred.

Multiple Scenes...

Investigators must collaborate closely with the medical examiner during the course of investigating a death related to a sexual assault. There will be instances where multiple scenes will be associated with the case, leading to the scene of the terminal event. The importance of identifying each related scene is crucial to examining the violent course that the offender took during the time they were with the victim. Once these various scenes are identified, crime-scene protocols must be adhered to strenuously. It is during this period of the investigation that evidence can be observed, documented, and collected, that can break open the investigation. The briefing during this phase between the lead investigator, crime-scene technician, and the medical examiner is crucial prior to the processing of the scene(s). When multiple crime scenes are identified, it is paramount that each scene be thoroughly examined and briefings between investigators and units or agencies, which are assisting, be conducted. The reasoning is very simple, evidence that is located in one scene may be found in another, thus creating cross-contamination between the scenes in question. These factors are critical and can be the determining factors in solving the case. The ability to show these pieces of evidence to a jury goes a long way in securing a guilty verdict.

The more evidence collected that shows a pattern of conduct by an offender, the easier it becomes for the prosecution to walk a jury through what a victim had experienced prior to the terminal event. Additionally, as multiple scenes are processed, there may be evidence that needs to be collected or just needs to be documented. The determination for either must be collaborated between the investigator, crime-scene technician, and the medical examiner. This is to ensure consistency with the collection process and with future testimony.

It is important to attempt to identify which is or was the initial scene related to the death of the victim. The scene does not always have to be physical (house, car, etc.) in nature. In today's world of cyberspace, internet sites and social media maybe areas where the offender and victim were connected. Another point to consider is the location where the victim is found and if that location was the initial location of the attack. An investigator must keep an open mind when investigating cases involving a sexual attack that resulted in a death, an important reason is, the victim cannot be interviewed and physical evidence becomes a crucial part of the investigation. Therefore, when conducting such an investigation, it is important to keep the medical examiner apprised of additional information pertaining to the location or website where the initial encounter or attack took place. This information will assist the medical examiner as they conduct their investigation.

Historically, in many homicide cases where the victim was attacked in one location but discarded or located at another, the timeline of events is crucial in determining where the initial violent event occurred. Additionally, with multiple crime scenes and a plethora of evidence to examine, the investigator must realize that the most crucial piece of evidence is the victim. The victim will be able to yield valuable amounts of cross-contamination or transfer-evidence upon the physical examination conducted by the medical examiner. These bits of trace evidence will be documented and collected for testing at the police lab. The results from the tests will assist in determining where and time the incident occurred. Investigators must understand that the procedure of collecting evidence from a victim's body must be performed in a sterile environment (morgue/hospital) and not in the field. Collection protocols must be adhered to and the crime-scene technician must be present to ensure proper procedures have been met. Once the victim has been photographed in the scene, the investigator must consult with the medical examiner in order to determine if the on-scene physical examination will be conducted or if the victim is to be transferred to the medical examiner's office (morgue). The reasoning for this strict procedure is to maintain consistent *chain of custody.*

As a lead investigator assigned to a death investigation where a violent sexual attack was committed, which precipitated the terminal event, it becomes extremely clear as to how important it is to securing the crime scene. Although crime-scene protocols were discussed in the section pertaining to crime-scene procedures, it can never be stressed enough the importance of securing a crime scene or multiple scenes for that matter.

Therefore, while investigating a death because of or connected to a violent sexual attack, an investigator must consider the possibility of multiple or overlapping crime scenes. It is also important to consider elapsed time of when the incident took place to when the victim was located. Another aspect is the type of paraphilia that could be associated with the victim's demise. An investigator must be deliberate in determining the type of paraphilia related to the investigation in order to proceed accordingly. It is during this stage that one must determine with a consensus of the crime-scene investigator and the medical examiner, what best practice to use in documenting and processing the crime scene. At this point, a determination will be made to process the victim while on the scene or to transport the victim to a sterile environment for processing. During this phase of the investigation, documentation is crucial, and nothing should be left undone. It is better to have more documentation that may not be needed than less documentation with missing evidence that is valuable. The investigator must be thoughtful when considering what items or evidence will be collected by the crime-scene technician. Items that should be considered for collection when investigating a death related to a sexual attack may be pornography, sex toys, bondage materials (handcuffs, tape or restraints), and recordings from cameras or tape machines. There are also the obvious pieces of evidence such as weapons, drugs, or alcohol. In scenes related to a violent sexual attack, crime-scene integrity and security is paramount in order to properly investigate the incident and to bring about a positive result. The investigator must ensure that the victim's body is properly prepared prior to being transported from the scene to the morgue. The victim should be transported in as an exact state as it was found.

Once the crime scene is processed and prior to releasing it, the investigator must debrief the medical examiner and the crime-scene technician. During this debriefing, ideas will be exchanged as to how better proceed from this point or if there is any need to keep the crime scene secured until such time that everyone involved with the investigation is satisfied with what has been accomplished. The investigator must keep in mind that if the scene was processed and secured through a search warrant, once the crime scene is released, one cannot return unless another search warrant is obtained. Additional evidence can be obtained because of techniques used by the medical examiner during the postmortem. As the lead investigator or a surrogate that attends the postmortem, it is crucial to ask questions of the medical examiner in order to get a better understanding of the evidence collected from the victim.

In conclusion, it is important for investigators to understand the complex nature of deaths resulting from a violent sexual attack and how many of these cases have multiple crime scenes that may be related to the terminal event. The investigator must have a basic understanding of the paraphilias associated with sexual deviancy when investigating sexual-related death cases. Knowing the basics of sexually related deaths, an investigator can determine what items must be collected as evidence and how a victim should be prepared prior to transportation from the crime scene to the morgue. There are so many approaches that can be employed by an investigator that it would take many years of continuous exposure to these types of cases in order to become proficient. Therefore, the responsibility of the investigator is to continuously study cases and attend seminars or medicolegal classes that will assist them in becoming a better investigator. Throughout an investigator's career, they will come in contact with a multitude of death cases which require detailed and thoughtful examination in order to achieve a positive result. Not all death investigations are of the criminal nature, but it is important for the investigator to have a general understanding of the mechanism of death. Various types of death cases were reviewed in this section, most are the ones that are commonly investigated, but there are many others that an investigator may never have a chance to investigate for a myriad of reasons. It is for this reason that if an investigator wants to excel in his or her profession (homicide investigator), then they must forge a bond with the medical examiners and be present at as many postmortems as possible, ask many questions, and attend seminars or any Medicolegal courses that are available. This section was written as a guide to assist the investigator develop a relationship with the medical examiner and was not intended to make the investigator an expert. In over 20 years of actively investigating death cases and mentoring aspiring investigators, I can state that I am still learning and willing to listen to other points of view. An investigator never stops seeking knowledge, the day that happens, it is time to get off the train.

Bibliography: V.J. Geberth – 2003 Sex-Related Homicide and Death Investigation: Practical and Clinical Perspectives. W.U Spitz and D.J. Spitz – Medicolegal Investigation of Death, 4th ed. Dr. David Dolinak, Dr. Evan Mathes and Dr. Emma O. Lew – Forensic Pathology, Principles and Practices

Chapter 4
State Attorney's Section

The alliance developed between an investigator and the state attorney's office, as well as the state attorneys that will be assigned to prosecute your cases, is crucial in order to bring a case to trial. The legal aspects of an investigation are fundamental components in order to affect an arrest of an individual or individuals that have been linked by various means to a homicide investigation. As an investigator, you must examine every aspect of a case in order to provide the best possible answers as to who, what, where, when, and how a violent incident, such as a homicide, took place. It is also the responsibility of the investigator to follow every lead possible and never leave a lead by the wayside. An investigator must remember that they are to investigate each case thoroughly and objectively. Investigations should never become personal when justice is the ultimate goal, which it is. Investigators need to understand that during the course of investigating a violent incident, evidence may be obtained that clears a possible suspect or subject, thus, this exculpatory evidence needs to be brought to light in order for justice to be served. An investigator's reputation carries a lot of weight as relationships are developed with the judicial system. It is better to delay making an arrest until such time that additional evidence has been developed, as opposed to making a hasty arrest and later finding out that a wrong person had been jailed (removal of one's freedom). Investigators should never be in a hurry to make an arrest; they should be slow and methodical, in order to present the best case in trial. Therefore, a good working relationship must be developed during the course of an investigation, between the investigator and the prosecutor assigned to assist, in order to expedite any legal aspects of the investigation.

It has been my privilege to work with dedicated professionals assigned to the Miami-Dade State Attorney's Office. With their guidance, I have been able to obtain a better understanding of the law, its power, and how to responsibly use it in order to bring about positive results during the course of an investigation. Attorneys such as David Waksman, Gary Winston, Gail Levin, Michael Van Zampft, Alejandra Lopez, Frank Ladee, and Abe Lasser were positive influences in my career. Their willingness to impart their knowledge of the law allowed me to have a better understanding of how vehemently cases are to be investigated in order to achieve a successful prosecution. An investigator is not going to earn a Juris Doctorate from reading this section, but it will help develop a good understanding of what is needed (legally) to successfully investigate a violent crime, or any other crime for that matter.

How can we properly investigate a crime if we do not respect the law? Are we above the law, that we change the rules in mid-investigation? As an investigator, one cannot change the facts to fit the crime; on the contrary, the facts will always lead you down the right path, whether or not you solve the case, or it remains open until such time that additional evidence has been uncovered.

During the course of an investigation, investigators will develop enough intelligence and get that gut feeling that a particular individual is their culprit. Except, there is not enough to apprehend the suspect. In arresting this suspect without enough probable cause (P.C.), just to get a clearance (even if the state attorney refuses to file the case), does the end justify the means? Did the investigator act in good faith? As a true professional, it is crucial to have a very good understanding of the state laws pertinent to violent crimes or any other crimes where one wants to excel. An investigator needs to become a quasi-expert in state laws of the U.S. Constitution, and the Bill of Rights, such as the Fourth Amendment and Fifth Amendment. Probable-cause issues come into play on various types of cases. So, how does an investigator approach the questions that arise during the course of an investigation, when evidence points in one direction and your gut tells you something different? The investigator needs to be meticulous during the course of an investigation, and perform his/her job in a correct manner, not what is expedient in order to appease those in higher command positions that will never testify in a trial. The investigator must *always do what is right* and not succumb to pressure or for the empty satisfaction of making an unjust arrest, just to clear a case. This will always come back to haunt the investigator and the agency they work for.

In order to become competent in your chosen field (death investigations or violent crimes investigations), let us review the statutes that will be an investigator's guiding light. Investigators must have a complete understanding of the laws associated with the crimes they are investigating, in order to prepare an excellent case for trial. In preparing to conduct an investigation, understanding these statutes allows for a better exchange of ideas or strategies with the state attorney assigned to the case. The following statutes are located in the Florida Law Enforcement Handbook. Keep in mind, other states have their own handbooks.

Before the statutes are reviewed, let us look at the legal difference between *murder* and *homicide.* Though murder and homicide are interchanged, there is a difference between the two. *Homicide* is the killing of a human being by another. Whereas, *murder* is related to a form of criminal homicide, where the perpetrator intended to kill the other person, sometimes with premeditation (offender planned to kill). Manslaughter is another kind of criminal homicide. Homicides are classified as criminal, excusable, or justifiable. A criminal homicide is unjustified and can result in severe consequences. When investigating a justifiable or excusable homicide, these incidents occur without criminal intent to kill someone. Self-defense, killing someone in the defense of another, or a law-enforcement officer who kills someone in the line of duty are examples of excusable or justifiable homicide. Murders are classified differently based on the severity of the crime and the offender's intent. Murders are classified as 1st degree, 2nd degree, 3rd degree or manslaughter. There are states that do not use 3rd degree. 1st degree murder needs the elements of premeditation and cruelty with afterthought. These state that the killing may not have been intentional, but it happened during the course of a crime, in such cases, consideration would be given to charge the offender for 1st degree murder. Investigators must remember that 2nd degree murder does not show a premeditation, and manslaughter occurs when the offender intended to harm, but the act resulted in death. Now, let us proceed to the statutes.

Florida Statute Book – Chapter 782, Homicide, 782.04, Murder. (1) (a) The unlawful killing of a human being: (2018)

1. When perpetrated from a premeditated design to affect the death of the person killed or any human being; **2**. When committed by a person engaged in the perpetration of, or in the attempt to perpetrate, any: **a**. Trafficking offense prohibited by s. 893.135(1) **b**. Arson **c**. Sexual battery **d**. Robbery **e**. Burglary **f**. Kidnapping **g**. Escape **h**. Aggravated child abuse **i**. Aggravated abuse of an elderly person or disabled adult **j**. Aircraft piracy **k**. Unlawful throwing, placing, or discharging of a destructive device or bomb **l**. Carjacking **m**. Home-invasion robbery **n**. Aggravated stalking **o**. Murder of another human being **p**. Resisting an officer with violence to his or her person **q**. Aggravated fleeing or eluding with serious bodily injury or death **r**. Felony that is an act of terrorism or is in furtherance of an act of terrorism; or **3.** Which resulted from the unlawful distribution of any substance controlled under s. 893.03(1), cocaine as described in s. 893.02(2)(a)4, opium, or any synthetic or natural salt, compound, derivative, or preparation of opium, or methadone by a person 18 years of age or older, when such drug is proven to be the proximate cause of death of the user, is murder in the 1st degree and constitutes a capital felony, punishable by imprisonment for a term of years not to exceed life or as provided in s. 775.082. (b) In all cases under this section, the procedure set forth in s. 921.141 shall be followed in order to determine sentence of death or life imprisonment. (2) The unlawful killing of a human being, when perpetrated by any act imminently dangerous to another and evincing a depraved mind regardless of human life, although without any premeditated design to effect the death of any particular individual, is murder in the 2nd degree and constitutes a felony of the 1st degree, punishable by imprisonment for a term of years not to exceed life or as provided in s. 775.082, s. 775.083 or s. 775.084.

There are additional statutes that cover other types of homicides; **782.02** Justifiable use of deadly force, **782.03** Excusable homicide, **782.051** Attempted felony murder, **782.065** Murder of any L.E.O., Correctional Officer or Correctional Probation Officer, **782.07** Manslaughter; aggravated manslaughter of an elderly person or disabled adult, aggravated manslaughter of a child, aggravated manslaughter of an officer, firefighter, an emergency medical technician, or paramedic. **782.09** Killing of unborn child by injury to mother. Then there is a very interesting statute **782.035** Abrogation of common-law rule of evidence known as *'year and a day rule.'* This statutes reads, the common-law rule of evidence applicable to homicide prosecutions known as the 'year and a day rule,' which provides a conclusive presumption that an injury is not the cause of death or that whether it is the cause cannot be discerned if the interval between the infliction of the injury and the victim's death exceeds a year and a day, is hereby abrogated and does not apply in the state of Florida. These statutes are best reviewed during an investigator's tour of duty and should be carefully studied when taking training courses in criminal law. All investigators should make it a point to become good friends with attorneys assigned to the state attorney's office in order to ask questions that will assist them in future investigations. Another piece of advice, know the local defense attorneys and ask them questions. As an investigator, it is always great to investigate a homicide as if working for the defense. Why? Because you will be better prepared for any questions that may arise during a deposition.

A police officer has the power to take away one's freedom. That power needs to be harnessed and unleashed when legally authorized. As a violent crime investigator, it is their responsibility to go beyond probable cause (P.C.) when effecting an arrest. An investigator should overturn every rock imaginable in order to discover the truth of what took place, prior, during, and after the violent event occurred. In doing this, an investigator just might uncover exculpatory evidence that can ensure a person is not unjustly arrested or prosecuted. An investigator must approach each investigation by this standard. One must investigate each case to the fullest as if one was trying to assist the suspect in beating the charge(s). In doing this, an investigator can rest assured that all efforts were taken in order to successfully get to the truth. Justice Louis Brandeis in his dissenting of *Olmstead v. U.S., 277 U.S. 438 (1928)* stated; *In government of laws, existence of the government will be imperiled if it fails to observe the law scrupulously. For good or for ill, it teaches the whole people by its example. Crime is contagious. If the government becomes a lawbreaker, it breeds contempt for the law; it invites every man to become a law unto himself; it invites anarchy.* It is for this precise reason; every investigator must be held to the highest standards and that should be without contestation. In addition, Justice Oliver Wendell Holmes, also dissenting in Olmstead, stated; *The government ought not to use evidence obtained by criminal act. We must consider the two objects of desire, both of which we cannot have and make up our minds which to choose. It is desirable that criminals should be detected, and to that end that all available evidence should be used. It also is desirable that the government should not itself foster and pay for other crimes, when they are the means by which the evidence is to be obtained.* The Honorable

Oliver Wendell Holmes felt that it was better to have a criminal escape arrest, temporarily, than to arrest a criminal by a dishonorable act. These principles were the foundations by which the United States Supreme Court, in *Mapp v. Ohio, 367 U.S. 643 (1961)* made the Fourth Amendment binding to the States. Therefore, an investigator must be extremely familiar with the U.S. Constitution, especially the Fourth Amendment.

Investigators must feel comfortable when dealing with the law and when explaining their position with the assistant state attorney assigned to the investigation. Most of the time, investigators will be asked how evidence was obtained. It is the investigators' obligation to ensure that nothing nefarious is done to obtain evidence. Investigators, no matter how good the intentions may be, should never collect evidence without proper authorization. Doing this will bring about dire consequences, both to the case and the integrity of the investigator. An investigator might come across an incident where evidence is collected before a search warrant or consent to search is secured. These issues will be studied throughout this chapter. As a violent crime's investigator, one must understand what is unacceptable at a scene of a crime, but most importantly, at the scene of a homicide.

DEPARTMENT OF POLICE

CITY OF (NAME), FLORIDA

C2

CONSTITUTIONAL RIGHTS – SEARCH BY CONSENT

BEFORE ANY SEARCH IS MADE, YOU MUST UNDERSTAND YOUR RIGHTS.

(1) YOU MAY REFUSE TO CONSENT TO A SEARCH AND MAY DEMAND THAT A SEARCH WARRANT BE OBTAINED PRIOR TO ANY SEARCH OF THE PREMISES DESCRIBED.

(2) IF YOU CONSENT TO A SEARCH, ANYTHING OF EVIDENTIARY VALUE SEIZED IN THE COURSE OF THE SEARCH CAN AND WILL BE INTRODUCED INTO EVIDENCE IN COURT AGAINST YOU.

I HAVE READ THE ABOVE STATEMENT OF MY RIGHTS AND AM FULLY AWARE OF THE SAID RIGHTS.

I HEREBY CONSENT TO A SEARCH WITHOUT WARRANT BY OFFICERS OF THE CITY OF (NAME) POLICE DEPARTMENT OF THE FOLLOWING.

(DESCRIBE PREMISES OR AUTOMOBILE)

I HEREBY AUTHORIZE THE SAID OFFICERS TO SEIZE ANY ARTICLE, WHICH THEY MAY DEEM TO BE OF EVIDENTIARY VALUE.

THIS STATEMENT IS SIGNED OF MY OWN FREE WILL WITHOUT ANY THREATS OR PROMISES HAVING BEEN MADE TO ME.

____
SIGNATURE OF SUBJECT

____
DATE/TIME

____
WITNESS

____
WITNESS

It is important to know what a *search warrant, probable cause,* and *Miranda Rights* are. These three topics are crucial during the course of an investigation. What keeps an investigator from acting on their gut feeling about a suspect? Without probable cause, can a suspect be arrested? Did they commit the crime or did they?

In reviewing the Fourth Amendment to the Constitution of the United States, it tells us;

The right of the people to secure their persons, houses, papers, and effects, against unreasonable searches and seizures, shall not be violated, and no warrants shall issue, but upon probable cause, supported by oath or affirmation, and particularly describing the place to be searched, and the persons or things to be seized. How wonderful is this amendment which our ancestors had the vision to create as part of our Constitution, which is in the Bill of Rights. Inside this amendment, an investigator begins to understand *probable cause* and *search warrant*. The Fourth Amendment case-law deals with three issues; those issues are what government activities constitutes *search* and *seizure,* and what constitutes *probable cause.* An investigator should also be aware of the term, *nexus.* If an investigator cannot establish a link or nexus of a crime to a person or place, then there is no probable cause to obtain a search warrant.

Now, a new investigator might have the gumption to ask their mentor, why must probable cause be established? Why bother with having to go before a judge to get a search warrant? At the end of the day, investigators want to do their job and get the subject. That is fine, but currently, not like in Old England (where the king ordered soldiers to search homes and businesses without a search warrant), an investigator must develop probable cause in order to go before a judge and swear or affirm that they have enough evidence that will allow for a legal search. As an understanding, in England, agents of the government were allowed to make as many searches as they wanted on businesses and homes. Then, in 1696, parliament authorized this same practice to take place in the colonies which were under English rule.

It was the abuse of this governmental power, both in England and in the colonies that created the impetus for the founding fathers to add language to the Fourth Amendment that would stop government entities from violating a person's privacy.

In the Fourth Amendment, a key question asked is whether a *search* took place. Investigators must keep in mind that Fourth Amendment case-law was reference to a citizen's property rights. This is when the government (law enforcement) physically intrudes on persons, properties, documents, or personal effects in order to obtain information, in this vein, a search has occurred. Investigators need to understand that an illegal search has occurred when the government (law enforcement) has violated a person's *reasonable expectation of privacy.* In the majority opinion written by Justice Potter Stewart, *Katz v. United States 389 U. S. 347 (1967),* he lets us know that the Fourth Amendment protects people, not places. However, in *Katz,* the expectation of privacy provided the basis in ruling that government intrusion, though electronic and not physical, was a search covered by the Fourth Amendment. Though this case was in reference to a wiretap, one can see why the court opined the way it did, thus, if an investigator has the nexus, it is reasonable to believe that a search warrant will be granted. The decision in this case was the impetus for the adoption of the two-pronged test; 1 – that a person 'has exhibited an actual (subjective) expectation of privacy' and 2 – society is willing to recognize that this expectation is (objectively) reasonable, *Smith v. Maryland (1979), 442 U.S. 735.* This test was adopted by the court in Smith.

In the Fourth Amendment, the unreasonable *seizure* of any person, person's home (including the curtilage), or personal property without a warrant is an important premise. This can occur when a person is in possession of property, which they feel they have the right to have, and a government official (law enforcement officer) takes said property away to use as evidence against the person. Investigators need to understand that though this amendment covers a person's freedom, when being detained (seized) by physical force, their freedom of movement is restrained or when a reasonable person feels they are not free to leave, *United States v. Mendenhall (1980), 446 U.S. 544.* If an investigator is questioning persons at a crime scene, but they are able to walk away (not ordered to stay), this contact is referred to as a 'citizens encounter,' *Florida v. Bostick (1991), 501 U.S. 429.* Because there is no seizure of the person, it does not fall under intrusion of a person's privacy.

There are *exceptions* to the Fourth Amendment, when the need of society is great, there are no other means of meeting with people at a crime scene, and the intrusion of the person's privacy is minimal. Though this applied toward motorist, in *Illinois v. Lidster (2004), 540 U.S. 419,* the Supreme Court allowed focused informational checkpoints. For the purposes of an investigation, it would make sense that an investigator can make contact with people at a crime scene, question them as part of an informational checkpoint during the course of the investigation.

As we discuss modern day investigations, the Fourth Amendment is paramount; there is a section that prohibits *unreasonable searches and seizures* and there is a *warrant clause*. An investigator does not always need a warrant. There are exceptions allowed by the courts. I am always reminded of something that was taught to me early on in my homicide career. A victim has the expectation that one will do everything legally possible to solve their case. Legally possible, not do what you want. There may come a time when an investigator is faced with the possibility of losing evidence because of pressure to clear a crime scene as soon as possible or collect evidence expediently. This rush will do nothing for the case other than allowing the subject to walk free. So, back to the exceptions. The courts have ruled that based on necessity or imminent danger to the police, exceptions are allowed. Most of these circumstances deal with moments when officers or investigators do not have the ability or opportunity to author a search warrant and present it to a judge based on the circumstances.

A search pursuant to a lawful arrest and the location within the subject's immediate control. This is known as the *arm's reach* or *wingspread case*. This ruling was derived from the case of *Chimel v. California, 395 U.S. 752 (1969).* This ruling is intended to ensure the safety of the officers and not to exceed into areas not reasonably believed to pose a threat. It is also intended to prevent the destruction of evidence. *Hot pursuit of a fleeing felon* is another similar rule, such as *Warden v. Hayden, 387 U.S. 294 (1967).* This was a case in Baltimore, Maryland, where two cab drivers witnessed a robbery and followed the offender to a house. They gave officers a description of the offender and what he was wearing. Based on the information, the officers were given permission by the woman who answered the door to enter and search for the offender. During the search, the offender (Hayden) was found in a bedroom, on a bed, acting as if he were asleep. Other officers located clothes matching the clothing description that was provided to them, as well as several weapons and ammunition. Although this seemed like an overreach by the officers, the court ruled that this was not an illegal search.

Based on the exigent circumstance of the case and the situation, the court allowed it. In this case, the main issue was that the search and seizures was conducted within minutes of the robbery having taken place. The court allowed the officers broad scope of the search in an effort to locate a violent felon who was armed and with the ability to get away.

Search to prevent the imminent destruction of evidence. This was a case reviewed by the U.S. Supreme Court, *Schmerber v. California, 384 U.S. 757 (1966).* This ruling dealt primarily with the taking of a subject's blood. Because, according to Justice William Brennan, it would be reasonable to determine that evidence (alcohol) in the blood will begin to diminish shortly after the individual stops drinking and the body begins to eliminate evidence. Extensive intrusion, such as pumping a subject's stomach to retrieve possible evidence, goes way beyond the purview of reasonable intrusion. **Note:** According to Justice Brennan, "The test performed in a reasonable manner… We hold today that the constitution does not forbid the states minor intrusions into an individual's body under stringently limited conditions and in no way permits more substantial intrusions." This ruling is geared mostly toward traffic homicide investigations and D.U.I. cases.

The plain view doctrine relates closely to the Fourth Amendment and what is considered to be reasonable for seizing evidence. Investigators should become familiar with this doctrine and review case law, *Ker v. California, 374 U.S. 23 (1963)* and *Coolidge v. New Hampshire, 403 U.S. 443 (1971)* (not really a search exception, just a reason to seize evidence). It was the court's opinion that, the plain-view doctrine is not in conflict with the first objective because plain view does not occur until a search is in progress. In each case, this initial (entry) is justified by a warrant, or by an exception such as hot pursuit or search incident to a lawful arrest, or by (another) valid reason for the officer's presence. In addition, given the initial lawful intrusion, the seizure of an object in plain view is consistent with the second objective, since it does not convert the search into a general or exploratory one. Therefore, if an officer sees evidence in plain view after obtaining permission to be where he is, the evidence can be lawfully documented and taken into custody (seized).

The automobile exception is linked to *Carroll v. United States, 267 U.S. 132 (1925)* and *Chambers v. Maroney, 399 U.S. 42 (1970)*. In reviewing these cases, an investigator needs to become familiar with the power that they possess. It is clear that all you need to search a car is probable cause, to believe its contents offend the law. The requirement of exigent circumstances is satisfied by the 'ready mobility inherent in all automobiles that reasonably appear to be capable of functioning, 'it is clear…that there are only two questions that must be answered in the affirmation before (you) may conduct a warrantless search of an automobile. First, is the automobile readily mobile? All you need to prove is that the automobile is operational. Second, probable cause, is determined under the facts of each case *United States v. Watts, 329 F.3 1282 (11th Cir. 2003)*. In a continued conversation of vehicles, we have the *inventory search (of a vehicle taken into police custody for safekeeping)*. This is a very easy way to conduct a legal, warrantless search. In *South Dakota v. Opperman, 428 U.S. 364 (1976),* the basic premise was ruled that if a driver of a vehicle is arrested, injured, or unable to take care of his property or if the vehicle is going to be towed for other reasons, one must protect it. During this process, officers must inventory the vehicle and document everything that was found inside. Items that are located must be secured; this ensures that if the driver makes a claim of a missing item, there is documentation of what was secured. Since the vehicle cannot be left unattended, it will be towed to the impound lot and the driver will be given an inventory list of what was found. **Note:** if evidence is located, such as weapons, narcotics, or other items pertinent to the case, they can be taken under the *Plain View Doctrine*. The investigator assigned to the case should have the lead crime-scene technician process the vehicle by documenting and photographing what was found and where in the vehicle was it located.

Stop and frisk is another valuable tool that can be used. Under *Terry v. Ohio, 392 U.S. 1 (1968),* the basic principle was, did Ofc. McFadden have justification for the invasion of Terry's personal security, by searching him for weapons in the course of that investigation? The immediate concern for the officer was, a possibility of a weapon being in the possession of the subject that could be unexpectedly used against the officer. Therefore, it is unreasonable to think that an officer would take risks in the performance of his duties. Especially when dealing with violent criminals. Recent history lets us know that many officers are killed or seriously wounded by criminals that have weapons hidden on their person. With this in mind, the opinion of the Court released in 1968 held; *the proper balance that has to be struck in this type of case leads us to conclude that there must be a narrowly drawn authority to permit a reasonable search for weapons for the protection of the police officer, where he has reason to believe that he is dealing with an armed and dangerous individual, regardless of whether he has probable cause to arrest the individual for a crime. The officer need not be absolutely certain that the individual is armed; the issue is whether a reasonably prudent man in the circumstances would be warranted in the belief that his safety or that of others was in danger.* Later cases would use the phrase *articulable suspicion.* With this, officers must testify to the court exactly what made him suspicious and why. Based on the officer's testimony, the court would determine if the officer's actions were justified. *Terry* should be reviewed thoroughly when dealing with *stop and frisk,* since there have been many cases after that the principles of *Terry* were invoked. One can review *Michigan v. Long 463 U.S. 1032 (1983),* this was a roadside encounter. The courts ruled that although the suspects were in handcuffs, they still remained a danger to the police, particularly when weapons are present. Additionally, "As an incident to the arrest, the officers could, as a precautionary matter and without probable cause or reasonable suspicion, look in closets and other spaces immediately adjoining the place of arrest from which an attack could be immediately launched." The court relied on *Chimel v. California, 395 U.S. 752 (1969)* for this response.

As a homicide investigator or violent crimes investigator, it is always great to search a location without a search warrant, really. The reason for this, it expedites the investigation and allows the lead investigator to release the location sooner, wow. Here is where the rubber meets the road for some supervisors, me included. Although it is the expectation of a victim for the investigator to solve the crime. I much rather go the extra mile and secure a search warrant, bingo. This ensures that all facts are authored by the lead investigator, and then presented to the assistant state attorney for final review before it is presented to a judge. Upon final review, the search warrant goes before a judge where the investigator attests to the facts that are in the body of the search warrant. Once the judge is satisfied with the *statement of facts,* the judge signs the search warrant. It cannot get any better than this, to know there will be no issues with evidence seized at the crime scene.

Nonetheless, let us have an understanding of a great tool during the course of an investigation, *consent search.* This ruling is based on *Schneckloth v. Bustamante, 412 U.S. 218 (1973).* This incident occurred in Sunnyvale, California, at three a.m., when Robert Bustamante agreed to let three officers search the trunk of his vehicle. The following was learned from this case: when the subject of a search is not in custody and the State attempts to justify a search on the basis of his consent, the *Fourth and Fourteenth Amendments* require that it demonstrate that the consent was in fact voluntarily given and not a result of duress or coercion, express or implied. Voluntariness is a question of fact to be determined from all the circumstances, and while the subject's knowledge of a right to refuse is a factor to be taken into account, the prosecution is not required to demonstrate (he knew he could say 'no'). Although one does not have to prove that the subject knew he had a right to say 'no' to the search, it is always best if the subject signs a *Consent to Search Form.* Once the subject signs the form, it becomes easier for the investigator when testifying in court. In general, the *Fourth Amendment prohibits warrantless entries* of a person's home, whether to make an arrest or to search for objects (evidence). That prohibition does not apply when a voluntary consent has been obtained from the person, *Schneckloth,* or from a third person having joint control over the premises. *United States v. Matlock, 415 U.S. 164 (1974),* during the course of an investigation and when investigators are formulating a course of action to proceed with a search, discussions take place where such things as *nexus* and *expectation of privacy* are debated. When *reasonable expectation of privacy* is reviewed, one must study *Katz v.*

United States 389 U.S. 347, at 352 (1967). Even though Katz is well *known* for establishing the concept of the *reasonable expectation of privacy,* that phrase was not found in the main opinion of the Court. Justice Harlan, in a concurring opinion, explained that, "I join the opinion of the Court, which I read to hold only that an enclosed telephone booth is an area where, like home… A person has a *constitutionally protected reasonable expectation of privacy.*" In citing Justice Harlan, the phrase, *reasonable expectation of privacy,* was officially created in *Terry v. Ohio.*

Now that several types of searches and seizures in the Fourth Amendment have been reviewed, let me impress upon veteran investigators as well as aspiring investigators of how important the next dimension becomes. All of the searches that you have just read about are important tools during the course of an investigation. Each tool has a purpose to a specific job; hence, we must keep these tools in our toolbox (memory). To me, the next dimension is the most important because it stops the investigator from making the crucial mistake of an unlawful search because of their zeal to collect evidence that will help them solve the case. It is always better to be slow and methodical, than fast and careless. Unless exigent circumstances dictate that evidence is to immediately be documented and collected, officers, upon securing the crime scene, *must stop* once the homicide or violent crimes investigators are called to assume responsibility of the investigation. Time is always on the investigators' side once the crime scene is secured. There is no reason for rushing the process, as previously stated; investigators could have valuable evidence excluded (*fruits of the poisonous tree*) because of wrongfully searching and seizing evidence. Above, the Fourteenth Amendment was mentioned and as a good investigator, you know that this amendment dealt with citizenship and it was adopted to the Constitution in 1868. Now, here is why the Fourteenth Amendment was mentioned. After the Civil War, this amendment to the United States Constitution was adopted in 1868 because many men of that period were concerned that when the South began to integrate with the North, they worried of the freed slaves' rights. The first section of the amendment was to revolutionize federalism. Know that this amendment mentioned the following: it stated that no state could 'deprive any person of life, liberty, or property, without due process of law; nor deny to any person within its jurisdiction the equal protection of the laws.' I hope that this gives the investigators a better understanding. The United States Constitution is a wonderful document and should be studied closely, it has much to offer.

This final dimension should be the rule that must be followed by investigators who work violent crime cases, but most importantly, homicides. Since early on in my career as a homicide investigator, I have been able to discuss cases and strategies with great state attorneys of the Miami Dade State Attorney's Office. These conversations allowed me to better understand the reasons why certain steps and strategies are used during the prosecution phase of a case. Nevertheless, the most important take from these conversations have been, what can an investigator do during the initial stages of an investigation to avoid losing valuable evidence before said evidence could be presented in trial. The more thought I gave to this principle, the more I remember discussing *Mincey v. Arizona* with a very good friend of mine, the late David M. Waksman, J.D. David always had a funny story to tell, having been a police officer in the South Bronx for six years and a very respected state attorney, in Miami, for over thirty years, he always managed to say the right things that would point you in the right direction. He never turned you away if you had a question and he always made you feel that you had something to contribute to the process of bringing about a positive result to the case at hand.

As investigators, let us review *Mincey v. Arizona, 437 U.S. 385 (1978)* and see how this case can be construed as the principles by which a homicide or violent crimes investigator should proceed during the initial stages of a violent and chaotic incident, where an investigator must keep their wits about them.

The facts of this case are as follows; on October 28, 1974, a narcotics officer, Barry Headricks, who was a member of the Tucson Metropolitan Narcotics Squad, arranged to purchase heroin from an individual named Rufus Mincey. During the course of Officer Headricks' investigation, he responded to the resident's (apartment) of Rufus Mincey with nine plain clothed officers and knocked on the door. An individual (John Hodgman), who was in the apartment with Mincey, opened the door. Once the door opened, Officer Headricks entered the apartment and went straight into the bedroom (where Mincey was). As the other officers entered the apartment, gunshots were heard coming from the bedroom. Officer Headricks exited the bedroom and collapsed on the floor; he died several hours later. The other officers that were in the apartment, found Mincey inside the bedroom, lying on the floor. Mincey was wounded and semiconscious, the officers searched the rest of the apartment for additional wounded persons. Mincey was transported to the hospital where the attending physician advised that Mincey sustained damage to his sciatic nerve, partial paralysis of his right leg, and was described as almost to the point of comatose. At some point after the initial incident took place, the homicide unit was requested to respond to the apartment in order to take over the investigation. An investigator at the hospital interrogated Mincey for several hours. Though Mincey requested counsel on several occasions, the investigator ignored the requests. During the initial stages of the investigation, the homicide investigators secured the apartment and searched it for four days. During the search, investigators processed the entire apartment without obtaining a *search warrant.* Eventually, the state charged Mincey with murder, assault, and three counts of narcotics offenses. The majority of the evidence introduced by the prosecutor was a direct result of the extensive search conducted by the officers inside Mincey's apartment. During the trial, Mincey's attorney contended that the evidence was unconstitutionally seized without a warrant and that the statements that he gave to the investigator were not voluntary, therefore rendering them inadmissible. During the preliminary hearing, the court found that *Mincey's statements were given voluntarily* and his motion to suppress the evidence that was seized from the apartment was denied. The Supreme Court of Arizona held that the warrantless search of Mincey's apartment was constitutional because it was a search of a homicide scene, and Mincey's statements were admissible for impeachment purposes, reversing the murder and assault on other grounds. Remember what was noted earlier, a victim has the expectation that one will do *everything legally possible* to solve their case. In this case, Justice Potter Stewart wrote, the Court held that the extensive, warrantless search of Mincey's apartment was unreasonable and unconstitutional under the Fourth and Fourteenth Amendments. *Justice Stewart further opined that warrantless searches were per se unreasonable with a few specific exceptions, and overruled Arizona's argument that the search of a homicide scene was one of these exceptions.* He further rejected Arizona's contention that Mincey forfeited his right to privacy in his home by shooting Officer Headricks. Justice Stewart wrote that this argument assumed Mincey's guilt and that the fact that Mincey was arrested did not remove his right to privacy in his home. He also rejected Arizona's position that the search of the homicide scene was justified by emergency circumstances or by vital public interests in prompt investigation of the scene. Justice Stewart further wrote; there were no exigent circumstances at the scene, allowing the search, and held that the seriousness of the alleged crime did not create those circumstances. Mincey's statements were ruled to be inadmissible because they were not given voluntarily since Mincey was in the intensive care unit, barely conscious and heavily encumbered by medical equipment when Detective Hust was interrogating him. The main focus of Justice Stewart surrounded Mincey's continued request for his lawyer that went unheeded. Investigators must remember that the Court opined that the four days of searching by the homicide investigators exceeded the exigent circumstances rule. In addition, there is no 'murder-scene' exception. There is no doubt that solving a murder as expeditiously as possible is of vital interest to the public, but that does not give law enforcements the authority to conduct warrantless searches of these types of investigations.

Reasoning logically, what sets a homicide apart from any other major crime such as robbery, aggravated battery, or rape? It does not, *GET THE SEARCH WARRANT!* In the case of Mincey, he was retried, convicted, and sentenced to life imprisonment. This case shed light during my career as to how a homicide investigation should be conducted. It further gave me a better understanding for mentoring the next generation of investigators. Understand, the court in Mincey did not say that the homicide investigators did not have reason to search the house, the court just wanted to let homicide investigators know that a search warrant was better suited. It is always great to fall in line with command staff that wants a quick resolution, but who takes the fall when the case goes south and it can, quick, if the investigator or the homicide team does not stand their ground. After Mincey, police officers that initially arrive at the scene of a homicide or other violent incident can only search for possible victims. *Once it has been determined that no other victims are inside the crime scene, the crime scene must be secured until a search warrant has been obtained.*

Investigators must have a great understanding of the rules and laws that apply to search and seizures. Knowing the principles for which the Fourth Amendment was drafted and why it is such a powerful tool only makes investigators better at their craft. It is the responsibility of investigators to use every tool at their disposal if they are to become experts in their chosen field. These principles that have just been reviewed are but a few of the ones that will guide investigators on a fulfilling journey on how to apply the law in order to bring about positive results on cases that are being investigated. Investigators will need to communicate with the assistant state attorney that is assisting with the investigation, not working, but assisting with the legal aspects that will allow for a better prosecution. An investigator can clear a case, but the case will not truly be closed until the offender is adjudicated *GUILTY.*

The investigator assigned as the lead has just concluded the search of the location where the incident took place, remember *search warrant.* The investigative team separated witnesses and a possible suspect, and they transported them to the criminal investigations section located at the police station in order to be interviewed by the investigative team. This is a simple procedure; witnesses were identified during the initial canvass of the crime scene and they freely agreed to assist with the investigation. Once at the police station, these good citizens should be kept as comfortable as possible. Remember, they are helping and do not have to do so if they do not want to. So, let us dabble into another one of those amendments, the *Fifth Amendment to the United States Constitution,* which is also part of the *Bill of Rights.* Reviewing this amendment now seemed appropriate, having just concluded with the *Fourth and Fourteenth Amendments.* In discussing the Fifth Amendment, investigators will better understand the term, *'pleading the Fifth'* and why Miranda Warning is afforded to a suspect.

Again with the history. The *Fifth Amendment to the United States* is the part of the *Bill of Rights* that protects individuals from being forced to be witnesses against themselves in a criminal case. That is why investigators and attorneys hear individuals say, "I plead the fifth!" all the time. This phrase lets one know that the individual declines to answer any questions that might incriminate them, and they do this knowing that they generally will not be penalized for exercising their right. This privilege ensures that a defendant cannot be forced to be a witness at his or her trial. However, if they do testify, this evidentiary privilege is no longer under consideration and they can be compelled to answer questions posed that are relevant to the case. This amendment is geared toward felonies only being tried once a *grand jury* grants a *True Bill of Indictment.* When a grand jury is convened in order to listen to testimony presented for a case, it normally involves what is considered an *'infamous crime,'* this type of crime is punishable by death if the defendant is convicted in trial. Federal grand juries are very different in that defendants can be compelled to take the witness stand, but they have the privilege to invoke the Fifth Amendment until they choose to respond to the questions they are being asked. So, what does this mean for defendants being interviewed by law enforcement? This means that the defendant can refuse to answer questions by invoking their Constitutional Right. This procedure is common when the investigating detective or officer advises the defendant of his or her *Miranda Warning.*

The fundamental basis for the *'Miranda Warning'* is to protect the defendant from being forced to self-incriminate himself or herself. 'Miranda' protects the *right to remain silent.* Other Commonwealth countries use this rule, which grants the right of defendants to remain silent both during questioning and at trial. This privilege protects innocent people from being charged by being deceived through abstruse circumstances. Remember, the Fifth Amendment was forged in order to limit the use of evidence illegally obtained by law enforcement officers, investigators, or patrol officers. The Supreme Court, siting that the confessions were illegally obtained, has overruled many convictions. One such case was *Brown v. Mississippi, 297 U.S. 278 (1936).* In this opinion by the Higher Court, it was determined that although law enforcement switched techniques to a subtler style, which did not involve physical torture, the new techniques that elicited an involuntary confession was ruled inadmissible. In another case, *Chambers v. Florida (1940) 309 U.S. 227,* Mr. Chambers was subjected to prolonged interrogation for five days, was not afforded the opportunity to have contact with anyone, and eventually confessed. The court held that such a technique to produce the confession was coerced and therefore, inadmissible. Another interesting case was *Ashcraft v. Tennessee (1944) 322 U.S. 143,* in this case, the defendant was interrogated for thirty-six hours straight under electric lights. The court held that prolonged interrogations where confessions are obtained under inherently coercive methods were inadmissible. Now that you have seen, a few of the decisions rendered by the higher court based on the methods used to elicit confessions, let us examine *Miranda v. Arizona (1966) 384 U.S. 436.*

In 1966, the Supreme Court renders their decision in *Miranda v. Arizona.* This decision established for future cases, that all suspects in criminal cases must be afforded their rights before being interrogated (we like to say interviewed). One does not have to be in law enforcement to know what 'Miranda Warnings' are. With all of the television shows dedicated to law enforcement, *Law and Order*, *N.Y.P.D. Blues*, and *Colombo*, just to name a few. I am sure that regular, everyday people know; 'You have the right to remain silent, anything you say can and will be used against you in a court of law.' These and the rest of the warnings are platitudes. So how did law enforcement get to this stage in the game? The Miranda incident took place on March 2, 1963, when an 18-year-old woman from Phoenix, Arizona, told police that she had been abducted, driven to the desert, and raped. The police followed leads based on a license plate number they had obtained, which matched a vehicle used by Ernesto Miranda, who had a prior record as a peeping tom. The victim never identified Miranda from a line-up, but they picked him up in police custody and brought him to the police station to be interrogated. According to the officers, Miranda, during the interrogation, confessed. Miranda recanted and was not aware that he did not have to say anything. The confession was brief and was different from the victim's account of events. During the trial, Miranda's appointed attorney called no witnesses and Miranda was convicted. While in prison, the American Civil Liberties Union took up his appeal, claiming that the confession was coerced. The Supreme Court overturned the conviction, but Miranda was retried in October, 1966, and convicted. Ernesto Miranda remained in prison until 1972 when ironically, he was stabbed to death in a men's bathroom in a bar, after a game of poker in January, 1976. This landmark case was the imputes for every suspect that is going to be questioned and arrested by police will be informed of their rights. Investigators must remember this, if you have not provided the suspect his or her 'Miranda Rights' and those rights were not waived, any evidence that was obtained during the interrogation becomes inadmissible.

Add the new Supreme Court ruling reference S.W. for cellphones (this is a hit to law enforcement).

Agency Police Department
Miranda Warning

BEFORE YOU ARE ASKED ANY QUESTIONS, YOU MUST UNDERSTAND THE FOLLOWING RIGHTS:

1. You have a right to remain silent and you do not have to talk to me if you do not wish to do so. You do not have to answer any of my questions. Do you understand that right?

   YES _____ NO_____

2. Should you talk to me anything which you might say may be introduced into evidence in court against you. Do you understand that right?

   YES _____ NO_____

3. If you want a lawyer to be present during questioning, at this time or anytime hereafter, you are entitled to have a lawyer present. Do you understand this right?

   YES _____ NO_____

4. If you cannot afford to pay for a lawyer, one will be provided for you at no cost if you want one. Do you understand this right?

   YES _____ NO_____

5) If you decide to answer questions now, without an attorney present, you will still have the right to stop answering at any time until you talk to an attorney. Do you understand?

   YES _____ NO_____

KNOWING THESE RIGHTS, ARE YOU NOW WILLING TO ANSWER MY QUESTIONS WITHOUT HAVING A LAWYER PRESENT?

YES _____ NO_____

THIS STATEMENT IS SIGNED OF MY OWN FREE WILL WITHOUT ANY THREATS OR PROMISES HAVING BEEN MADE TO ME.

YES _____ NO_____

____
Signature Date/Time

____
Advising Officer Date/Time

____
Witness Date/Time

Chapter 5
Interviews and Interrogations
A Psychological Approach of Conducting Interviews

The greatest asset that any investigator can have is the *'Gift of Gab.'* The following philosophies are a small sample taken from many years of experience and training. There is nothing better than to hold a conversation with people. As an investigator, you should be able to touch on a multitude of subjects and communicate with a diverse group of people. Why would this be important? If one thinks about how information is gathered, one gets a better understanding of how crucial communication is and its value to an investigator. As an investigator, or for that manner a layperson, would it not be great to hold a general conversation with anyone, anywhere? Investigators need to understand that their greatest asset is the way in which they communicate with others. It should not matter whom you are speaking with, it can be a doctor, lawyer, carpenter, student, child, mother, or father. The way in which you conduct the initial conversation or introduction, will set the tone for the remainder of your conversation. I like referring to the verbal or written interaction with others as *conversation or communication*, as opposed to *interviews and interrogations*, with respect to the investigator's interaction with people at a crime scene or in the police station. A general understanding of multiple topics is a fantastic icebreaker when trying to connect with a perfect stranger under difficult circumstances. An investigator should have enough confidence in their ability to communicate with anyone and at any time, in a moment's notice. This is where the *'Gift of Gab'* comes into play.

So, for the purpose of this chapter, let us explore avenues of how an investigator properly and effectively communicates with witnesses, family members, living victims, and most importantly, the suspect of the investigation. In understanding the methodology of *interviews and interrogations,* investigators will be well on their way in obtaining information that cannot be physically collected on a crime scene. The ability to extract information that is being withheld by a person, who is unwilling to part with it, can be challenging. Therefore, investigators must be extremely prepared to meet that challenge. One should review video clips of interviews – good and bad, in order to evolve.

As an investigation progresses, intelligence gathered at the crime scene can assist the lead investigator piece together what occurred, where it occurred, and possibly, when it occurred? However, the crucial bit of information which is missing at this point of the investigation is, who committed the crime and why was the crime committed? This is where the investigator must begin to develop rapport with potential witnesses, neighbors, surviving victims, and most importantly, family members. Investigators must know that people just do not want to speak with the police, no matter what. So, knowing this beforehand should prepare the investigator for the task of gaining people's trust. Investigators must navigate the path of developing trust, but the first way is through communication. Preconceived notions of people create an instant barrier that, at times, is hard to break. Investigators must open themselves to realizing that not everyone is like you. Many people who are exposed to investigators will have varied opinions of police officers, politics, racial animus, and just a general disposition of distrust (possibly created by a past negative experience with law enforcement). Therefore, it is the investigator's responsibility to bridge that gap by forging a path toward common ground. Bridging this gap is the foundation to obtaining the crucial information that will be needed in order to potentially solve the case being investigated.

Everything discussed to this point commences with communication and how effective the information gathered during the initial communication is to an investigation. For years, there has been debate over the manner in which information is obtained by investigators. Recently, during the confirmation hearings for the position of C.I.A. director, Gina Haspel, who eventually was sworn in as the new C.I.A. director, was questioned extensively with regards to her views of the techniques that were used on prisoners in order to gather information. Some senators on the committee grilled Gina Haspel as to her beliefs on whether or not aggressive techniques were valuable and justified, and also questioned her. These techniques, which are generally termed as Enhanced Interrogation Tactics, were used in the early stages of the war on terrorism after the 9/11 attacks. How effective were they? We may never know, but for the purposes of violent crimes investigations, rest assured that these types of techniques will never be used. My reason for saying this becomes clear when thinking of the early days of investigations when phonebooks, rubber hoses, and shiny lights were used in order to elicit a wanted response by the investigators, even if the subject was not involved. Thank God these are no longer the methods used!

Many of today's techniques are methods which have been formulated by psychologists. These techniques are geared toward a military application and really have no purpose in domestic cases. *Interrogations*, or as I like to call it, *conversations,* are conducted by law enforcement investigators, not military personnel. For domestic applications, interviews are conducted in a manner that is consistent with the rule of law governed under the U.S. Constitution. Can suspects' rights be violated even if they are known to have committed or been a part of the crime?

At what point does the investigator cross that line? This is a very simple answer. An investigator must never violate a suspect's rights, *Never ever!* Domestic interrogations are conducted by local, state, and federal law enforcement of witnesses or suspects with some sort of tie to a particular investigation. Investigators must follow the guidelines established by the U.S. government and the Supreme Court. The main reason for this rule to be followed becomes clear when defense attorneys argue the validity of the interview before the court, during proceedings leading up to trial. The manner in which any interview is conducted will be intensely litigated by lawyers; they will bring up facts regarding where the interview took place and how long the interview lasted. Investigators need to be trained in the various methodologies, behavior analysis, pathology that qualify a witness or suspect's mental competence for the interview, and how they will stand-up during trial. Persuading a witness or suspect to divulge crucial information must be done in a thoughtful manner that follows the strict guidelines set forth by the U.S. Constitution. Investigators must learn to play the cat and mouse game with those that are reluctant to disclose what information they know about a particular case. Patience and knowledge about a case is an investigator's biggest friend. Aggressive tactics during an interview plays no part in a local investigation. Investigators must be prepared to interview witnesses or suspects as if they were a long-lost friend and create a sense of comfort, not cause hostility, even under trying circumstances.

Most of the tactics used by local law-enforcement investigators are from the Reid Technique, which tend to befriend or offers' personal versions of information running from legal to illegal and/or manipulative to physical. This technique requires that suspects are assumed guilty until proven innocent, and the burden of proof is on the suspect. As an investigator, you must understand that the Reid Technique is considered by some to be somewhat questionable with its conflict within the judicial system, as well as the potential damaging effect it might have on those individuals being interviewed. In fact, this type of technique is potentially devastating to the case because the possibility of an investigator obtaining a false confession is about 25% (Malloy, Shulman, and Cauffman, 2014). Many psychologists deem this type of mental manipulation as being negative, even if many true confessions are obtained. In addition, interviews that are conducted with guilty suspects for lengthy periods, such as 24 hours or more, can cause psychological harm. Several studies have proven that the way in which the questions are presented in the Reid Techniques' seventh step of asking alternative questions can cause false memories in a suspect's neural pathway (Munsterberg, 2009; Shaw and Porter, 2015). Using certain phraseology in questions can give a suspect the idea that they did commit a crime or a witness that they did see a specific person commit a crime. Investigators must learn to stay away from leading questions that will elicit a positive response. An example of a phraseology question would be, "And when your father touched you, how did it feel?" This gave the person being questioned the inference that the father did touch them, when in fact, the act never took place. There have been cases where memories of crimes were created by manipulating an individual's memory based on background information and phrasing which caused the individual to give a false confession of a crime (Shaw and Porter, 2014).

Effective Techniques

The notion of interrogation, no matter how minimal, sends chills through the spine of those that do not understand what this tactic consists of. There are many ways that an investigator can approach the interview/interrogation, or as I like to call it, the conversation, with a subject or witness. Investigators must take under consideration how wide a scope they have when conducting the interrogation of a subject or when having a conversation with a possible witness. The approach and manner in which the interview is conducted can make or break the investigation. This wide range approach can create several physiological or semantic reactions by those being interrogated or interviewed. Whether they become withdrawn, combative, animated, and unable to understand simple words or the inability to logically express thoughts are indicators associated with individuals being interrogated or interviewed. Nervousness plays a big part of this reaction and one that investigators must detect. An aggressive style of interview, in many cases, can cause the subject to withdraw into a shell because of the initial shock of what is occurring. There have been studies performed in order to achieve the best practice possible for obtaining vital information through nonaggressive or invasive techniques. Such methods take years and dedication to perfect. Motivational interviewing or persuasive intervention by using familiar voice cadence are additional techniques that can be useful.

It would be highly unlikely that an investigator at the local level would ever utilize invasive techniques (current buccal swab), although most investigators use the Reid method where the subject is considered guilty first and innocent second. Prospect and attribution theories could apply when using a motivational style of interviewing. This style allows for the subject/suspect to deal with their guilt during the conversation they are having with the investigator and in doing so, they confess to the act. This result is directly related to the manner in which the investigator was able to develop a positive rapport and trust with the suspect/subject. Investigators must always keep in mind that the human rights, as well as the constitutional rights of the suspect/subject must always be at the forefront of the interrogation. What good does it do for the investigation if a confession was obtained by less than desirable means? Where does the reputation of the investigator or the agency lay, if this is what is allowed to happen? Nothing good comes because of these methods. It is incumbent upon the investigator and the investigative team to properly devise a game plan that will get the desired results, *legally.*

Undoubtedly, it is my opinion that a good interview/interrogation (conversation) is all psychological. There is no other way to put it. An investigator that is equipped with as much facts as possible, that has been gathered during the course of an investigation, has the upper hand when given the opportunity to interview a suspect/subject. Investigators must have a moral compass when conducting interrogations in order to avoid the pitfall of abuse during the course of an interrogation. For this reason, it has been suggested that there should be an independent investigator always monitoring the interview in order to properly balance the methods being used by the interviewer. The independent investigator can crosscheck the methods being employed in order to bring order to the interrogation and not allow it to get out of hand. It is true that all investigators want to successfully clear a case with an arrest and better still with a full confession, but what good does it do if the confession is stricken from court proceedings because of the maleficence of the investigator. Nothing good is ever gained from dishonest or unethical means.

The Strategy

Investigators must develop a game plan/*strategy* in order to properly conduct an interview/interrogation of a suspect/subject. During the course of a violent crime or homicide investigation, getting people to speak with an investigator is like pulling teeth, very difficult. In general, people avoid law enforcement at all cost, unless they are the ones that need them. In earlier discussion of the psychology of an interview, an investigator can deduce the difficulty of communicating with people that do not want to speak with you and as a non-psychologist, it would be difficult to know how to begin to speak with perfect strangers in order to gather vital information regarding the investigation at hand. The investigator needs to develop an effective strategy that will assist them during the course of an interview/interrogation. Remember, a good interview/interrogation is all psychological and the investigator must find that door which has been closed by the suspect/subject, find the key, and open it. This approach will determine in which direction the interview/interrogation will go.

As the lead investigator, it is your responsibility to be prepared. Investigators must gather as much intelligence as possible if they are to successfully interview a suspect/subject. Based on everything that was learned at the crime scene, investigators are able to establish an avenue for those they are about to interview. Upon entering the interview room, the investigator must exude a positive attitude, but not arrogant. Always remember, investigators were not present when the incident occurred, so do not try to 'bullshit' your way through an investigation. Investigators need to establish a rapport with the interviewee. They must find a way to break the ice. Basic information about the suspect/subject goes a long way. A simple question such as, "What is your name?" is a beginning. Then, you expand into other generalities that will give you a foundation, maybe it is not solid at this point, but your goal is to strengthen the foundation.

This simple task might seem easy, but it is not. There may be times when an investigator expends an enormous amount of time just to get an interviewee to reveal their name. In taking these first steps, investigators must develop a certain procedure that feels comfortable to them. Their approach should not be robotic; instead, it should flow freely and feel natural. Remember, suspects/subjects can sense if you are playing games and fishing for information.

The Guidelines

Now that the witnesses or suspect/subject has been transported to the police department in order to be interviewed, there is a type of strategy that needs to be utilized by the investigator. This dance began when the initial contact was made at the crime scene with the individual(s) that will be interviewed. The investigator's demeanor and initial impression sets the tone for how effective the remainder of the encounter will go. Establishing a good relationship with witnesses or suspect/subject is crucial in getting the investigation going in the right direction. Let the person(s) that will be interviewed know why they are going to be interviewed and why their help is important. Investigators must be nice, especially to those people with possible information that can assist with clearing an investigation. Confrontation should be used as a last resort; it is not always needed. Investigators must remember that witnesses are human and handle certain stressful situation differently. A witness can be highly agitated or nervous.

When an interviewer is speaking with potential witnesses, they need to keep perspective of what it is they are trying to extract from the witness. Witnesses can be fickle and reluctant to divulge information voluntarily, so good interviewers must make them feel comfortable and have them feel that they are a crucial part of the investigation. The interviewer's approach must be one of thoughtful consideration for what the witness has just experienced. A violent incident can trigger many emotions and feelings, and it is up to the interviewer to control the tempo of the interview. Interviewers do not want to ask leading questions or suggestive questions to those witnesses being interviewed. Interviewers need to document the raw response that a witness gives. Once this initial response is given, the interviewer must have enough information gathered from the initial canvass and scene processing to formulate follow-up questions. Investigators must take their time, be patient and diligent in order to extract as much information as possible. Remember that all people see and hear things differently. Each person that is interviewed is a piece of the puzzle and the information that they provide will allow the investigator to place it in the right spot of the investigation.

Investigators, through their years of experience, develop a style unique to how they are. An investigator's personality, preconceptions, and experience play a huge role in how an interview would be conducted. During my 25 years as a homicide investigator and supervisor, I was able to develop my own unique style based on my 'Gift of Gab.' It was always my contention that if I could engage a witness or suspect at any level or topic of conversation, my job as an interviewer would be made that much easier. As an outgoing individual, I have always practiced the art of striking up conversations with complete strangers in order to refine my skills as an interviewer. Remember how early on it was noted that an *interview/interrogation* was another way of saying *conversation*, except at a different level. It has always been suggested that all interviews should have a format to follow. For inexperienced investigators that will be conducting their first few interviews, I have always been of the school of sitting in with an experienced interviewer in order to pick up valuable tips.

Regardless of the type of investigation that is being conducted, whether homicide or any other violent crime, basic fundamentals and techniques of interviewing witnesses or suspect/subject should be consistent. When the approach is consistent, there can never be an issue as to why some interviews are conducted in one manner while others are done in another. Strategies may change during the course of an interview, which might cause a deviation with the approach, but the basic premise of the interview remains the same. In today's technological world, interviews are conducted in rooms that are video and audio recorded. These rooms are great, but there might be times when an interview cannot be conducted in such a sterile environment, so the old methods of tape recorders or stenographers come into play. "I cannot remember the last time I used a stenographer, wow! That tells you how ancient I am, but enough of my age." Investigators need to understand that *ALL* interviews must be memorialized so that there is no misunderstanding of what was said or how a question was asked and answered. Investigators must prepare themselves for a very long interview, whether of a witness or suspect/subject, in order to get a mental picture of how the interview's outcome will be. The outcome may not be how the investigator expected; on the other hand, it might be better.

An investigator's questioning must be such that each question posed is to elicit the proper response that gets you closer to the truth. The response may also set you further away from the initial premise. This is when the information that is in the investigator's possession becomes critical in discerning truth from lie. Responses to questions should be in almost chronological order based on location of the witness and at what point they entered the mix.

In the case of the suspect/subject, the responses may be for self-preservation and this is where the interviewer's prowess comes into play, being able to dissect what is being said and how it fits the narrative of the investigation. In today's world, the old-fashion way of having a statement written by the witness or suspect/subject is not really recommended, unless under exigent circumstances. Defense attorneys will always question the validity of written statements by the witness or suspect/subject as having been authored under pressure from the investigator. Investigators must take into account the educational level of the witness or suspect/subject that is writing a statement. If the educational level or mental faculty of the author is low, then everything that was written can be left up to interpretation. This will definitely create a problem which will be litigated before trial. For this reason, investigators must make every effort to ensure that statements are video and audio recorded. This method allows for clear and undisputed evidence as to how the witness or suspect/subject was treated, acting, and answering the questions. It immortalizes the statement and protects the investigator from being accused of unnecessary psychological or physical abuse.

Once a witness or suspect/subject agrees to be interviewed, time is on the investigator's side. There is no need to rush the process. Investigators need to have a game plan on how to approach the interview, because not every interview will be the same. The structure and method may be the same, but the interview itself might vary. Keeping the person that is being interviewed engaged is the key, and it is up to the investigator to avoid antagonizing the person. Remember, you want the witness or suspect/subject to talk as much as possible, but do not allow them to ramble on. Investigators need to know when to slow down an interview, when to take a break, and how to redirect the person to focus on the questions being asked.

All statements are important in order for the investigator to properly investigate and successfully close a case. Each statement is a piece of the puzzle and it paints a picture of the incident being investigated from a different perspective, depending on who is being interviewed. This is where the investigator must clean up what they learned from the interview as compared to the physical evidence of the crime scene. Witnesses that give detailed statements are a key indicator that they were present and have firsthand knowledge of what took place and possibly why. The investigator needs to keep in mind certain details that only a person who was present would know. Just like a confession, once the offender begins to confess to his or her participation in the violent act, specific details and motives clearly lets the investigator know that they have the person who committed the act. Only someone with intimate details of the incident can give specific descriptions of what took place, therefore ensuring that no details are fabricated.

It is the responsibility of the investigator to conduct a neutral and clean interview based solely on the facts and evidence. This is not to say that various strategies cannot be used, so long as they are always based on the facts and evidence.

Chapter 6
Team Leadership during an Investigation
Burden of Command

Beginnings of an Investigator's Leadership

During the course of any investigation, there will be instances when inexperienced investigators will be asked to command a major crime scene until such time that the on-call team responds or the primary investigator arrives at the scene. How is the inexperienced investigator going to manage the scene? How will the investigator take command of the scene, knowing that there is a chance that command-staff personnel might be present? This chapter is geared toward leadership during the course of an investigation and how to become better prepared for the burden of command.

The responsibility of any crime scene, no matter what type of crime has taken place, falls on the first investigator that arrives on the scene. In reality, it falls on the first officer until the investigator's arrival. Multiply that responsibility a hundred times over when the incident is a major crime such as a shooting, robbery, sexual battery, or a homicide, with multiple scenes and victims. Other incidents, although they might not be major in scope, are death investigations such as natural, accidental, unclassified, or suicide cases. These investigations are treated with the same amount of fervor until such time it can be determined, through investigative means that foul play did not occur. It is a great undertaking by the investigator on a scene to stay composed, delegate assignments, and ensure that the scene is secured until the primary investigative team arrives on the scene. An investigator's leadership comes into play, regardless of their experience. That is why every investigator must be mentally prepared to accept the responsibility of taking charge of any incident until such time that they are properly relieved.

Unfortunately, on many occasions, inexperienced command-staff personnel will arrive on such calls and begin to perform what I like to call, 'the curiosity dance.' Command staff will walk around, slowly at first, and begin to inch ever so closely to the main scene. Here is the tricky part. How prepared is the investigator, regardless of seasoning to stop 'command staff' or any unauthorized personnel from totally contaminating a crime scene? What happens when a 'command staff' member shows up on a scene, looking totally unprofessional (wearing a shower cap, sweatpants, under-armor shirt, and slippers)? It's happened!

In moments like these, an investigator better have the internal fortitude and confidence to confront such behavior professionally, and advise whoever showed up in such a manner that it is unbecoming and makes the agency, as well as the city they represent, look bad.

Investigators, like any other officer, has a chain of command that must be respected. The respect goes as far as the rank, unless the individual holding the rank has demonstrated such reverence that allows for the investigator in charge of the scene or investigation to carry on with the task at hand. It is times like these when *ALL* officers on a crime scene look to the investigator for their leadership in handling such unprofessional behavior. Unfortunately, during the course of investigating a major incident, investigators are so focused that they might come across as crass or disrespectful. That is far from the intention. During critical incidents, investigators, as well as their supervisors, are geared toward the solving of the incident at hand and, sometimes, responses are taken out of context. Then, you come across a younger generation of law-enforcement officers that are very sensitive to the way specific instructions are assigned or how an investigator responds to a question (usually asked at an inopportune time).

Investigators, upon their arrival on a major crime scene, cannot always wait for their supervisor to be present before taking charge. Leadership on a crime scene takes many forms and, sometimes, is displayed by the most unexpected officer. But leadership on a crime scene is a commodity that cannot be lost, stifled, or amputated. It must be nurtured and molded so that investigators feel empowered to perform their duties without being second-guessed. I have always been marveled at how often higher-ranking officers, who have never been in-charged of an investigation, profess to know about investigating cases and begin to dictate a course of action without knowledge. Unfortunately, they feel the need to impose their will on an investigator who has the responsibility of getting everything prepared, especially during a major crime investigation. It has always been amusing to me when I hear officers or command staff with no investigative experience say how much they did at another agency or how they were assigned to specific units and solved specific cases. In moments such as these, it takes discipline to allow such comments to be made and not respond. Why? Because there is a job that needs to be done and a case that must be solved.

Investigators cannot find themselves in a nonsense confrontation that will distract them from the task at hand. Investigators must acknowledge that they might come across officers or command-staff personnel that are present on a major incident, wishing they had the knowledge to successfully clear the case. These encounters are rare with large agencies, but are somewhat frequent with smaller ones. I have always enjoyed observing certain officers, regardless of rank, investigate vicariously through those that are actually investigating the case. Investigators need to understand that unfortunately, there might come a time during an investigation, where the politics of an agency or community comes into play. One must be prepared to deal with these challenges and overcome the petty squabbles of others.

Inexperienced investigators might be willing to step away from their responsibilities for fear of being admonished. There are experienced investigators that will do the same for fear of being transferred from a specific unit for standing their ground. Investigators need to realize that their presence and demeanor on a major crime scene is a soothing factor during a time of *CHAOS,* so long as they display command presence, enthusiasm, and *LEADERSHIP.* These traits should be applauded by those in positions that can impact the psyche of a young investigator for the remainder of their career. Investigators that are assigned to major crimes' units place themselves in leadership roles, whether they like it or not. Most investigators thrive in this role.

Effective Communication

On a crime scene, especially a major crime scene, effective communication is paramount in order to proceed with the investigation. The investigator in charge of the crime scene or investigation needs to understand whom they are communicating with. Investigators need to understand, the way in which they communicate with other investigators is not the same way they communicate with other officers, assisting entities, or civilians. Certain phrases or expressions might be interpreted differently depending on who is receiving the information or instructions. Investigators must be clear, direct, and give precise instructions. Instructions that are given cannot be lost in translation. Everyone must understand the gravity of the situation and the importance of their role, no matter how small (from logging in those that are present to writing down specific facts). An investigator's attitude on a scene goes a long way in getting things done quickly or reluctantly. They must get in a habit of listening before spewing orders. Do not allow *little* things to become *big* things for no reason. Patience and understanding goes a long way. Do not allow personalities to clash. Investigators can be firm, but calm with the delivery of their message.

Remember, officers and other investigators are looking at you for guidance. Also, command staff, as well as other supervisors, are taking note of your demeanor and how you are taking control or not of the incident at hand. Investigators, regardless of experience, must be prepared to ask the right questions, listen to the answers, and ask follow-up questions before responding. Sometimes, it is easier to step away from a situation before a response is given, even if the response is warranted. Have the right approach when speaking with others, remember that you are now in the middle of a hectic, violent crime scene, and emotions may be getting heated. People will respond more to the attitude that is perceived rather than the message that is given. A simple approach can change the dynamics of a potential violent situation at a crime scene.

An investigator's approach can defuse or incite any and all situations. Investigators need to recognize that a bad situation can yield a positive outcome if the right choices are employed. Throughout the course of an investigation, investigators must be themselves.

They cannot be phonies; they must stay true to their profession and the investigation at hand. Affected parties can always detect when an investigator is being disingenuous and this will always come back to haunt the investigator.

A Charismatic Approach

Leadership, during the course of an investigation, can come down to an investigator's charisma. An investigator's ability to inspire those around them through their charm and influence can garner enthusiasm and interest from those involved with the investigation. An investigator's charisma is infectious and the team usually gravitates to those that display such genuine passion. During the course of a lengthy and difficult investigation, a leader with energy usually galvanizes the team in order to achieve a successful conclusion. Although not every incident has a successful conclusion that does not mean that maximum effort was not put forth. The investigative team, as well as many surrounding the investigation, are focused on the lead investigator and his or her nonverbal demeanor. In saying this, I mean that facial expression and body language goes a long way to show approval or displeasure by the lead investigator. Investigators must be comfortable within themselves to be left vulnerable so that others can impart information or strategies and not feel as if they will offend or embarrass the investigator in-charge. A good leader must accept help from everyone without taking offense.

Investigators must avoid confrontation or conflict at all cost. During the course of a lengthy investigation, emotions can be charged and a good leader must be able to keep everyone cool and focused. Confrontation can turn any situation into a mess, no matter how small, confrontations are difficult to work around. Confrontations are a strain on a team's relationship and tends to divide each member. Now, there are times when confrontation is a healthy way to air out differences, so long as it is done in a respectful, thoughtful manner, and in the right situation. Leaders must understand that all team members want to have a successful conclusion to all investigations, and there will be times when emotions run high. Everyone's opinion must be accepted and the leader needs to listen to various points of view before they make the final decision. Leaders should not be overinvested in something that is minimal in comparison to the investigation at hand. Lead investigators must stay focused on the investigation, absorb all the information that is being relayed in order to make sound decisions. Being in conflict does not mean that the leader or lead investigator must be defensive about their decisions. They must stay steadfast and resolute. During these moments of being tried, if a leader flinches, *ALL* credibility is lost. Leaders must take risks during the course of any investigation, but they should provide an escape for those who might have had good intentions that were not sound. In doing this, the leader effectively allowed for a solution through compromise, while maintaining the integrity of the team and investigation intact.

Leaders must think like the units they lead, especially when they are in charge of a major crime investigation. It does not matter what rank is held by the lead investigator, they are there to lead their team and should expect each team member to perform at a high level. General George S. Patton once said, "Trying to lead men from behind makes you a driver and not a leader." A good investigative leader must allow for the investigative team to perform their job without micromanaging the team, but still have control of how the investigation is progressing.

This is true in every facet of a major crime investigation and the lead investigator that is leading the investigation. The lead investigator is not trying to solve a violent incident through popularity, they must focus on the mission at hand and direct those investigators assigned to assist, while making sure they, too, are focused. As a leader, the lead investigator needs to impress upon the investigative team that everyone assigned to the investigation has a vested interest in its success. I enjoy using the term, 'Attack the Castle,' which means to go out and give it your all until there is nothing left to give. A good leader knows the value and limits of each team member, as well as their own limits. During the course of a lengthy and difficult investigation, the lead investigator must know how far to push the team. Leaders should not overextend their team beyond their limits. In doing this, the investigation will suffer due to inefficiency and lack of productivity.

Challenges

Every major investigation possesses an enormous amount of challenges that must be confronted and dealt with by the lead investigator. How an investigator (no matter the experience) approaches each challenge will determine the effectiveness of their leadership abilities. The way in which an investigator chooses to lead during the course of an investigation can determine the effort or assistance that is given to them by others. Inexperienced investigators are, in essence, informal leaders, who might have experience as a patrol officer, and others around them will listen based on perceived experience and reputation. Not holding a rank allows you to opine and make suggestions that others will follow, even though your investigative experience is minimal. This can be a challenge because what the investigator says might be taken as gospel even though the instructions are unsound. Leaders face challenges throughout their career. Investigative leaders face challenges that hold dire consequences if their decision-making is weak. It takes years for an investigator to become completely confident with the decisions they make. This confidence comes from investigative experience, training, and a willingness to listen to other more-experienced investigators. Investigators must step out and accept that they do not know everything from investigating one incident and by the same token, experienced investigators continue to learn because they have not seen it all.

Every agency that has a major crimes section faces challenges of manpower, inexperience, communication, commitment, and accountability. Investigators must be able to overcome such obstacles if they want to succeed. New investigators, as well as senior investigators, must be empowered to complete their mission without being second-guessed by administrators. Investigative challenges come into play when investigators are intimidated by command staff or supervisors that lack experience to positively impact the case's outcome.

Responsibility

As a leader assigned to a major crime unit, your rank should not matter. The time that each investigator has put into learning their craft gives credence and legitimacy to their dedication and knowledge specific to the investigation being conducted. Remember, every investigator must have a starting point which is usually as a 'go-for' on any major crime unit. As investigators build up their credibility, they eventually move up the ladder of seniority within the team and the unit. Hopefully, well-trained investigators are able to ascend to where they become team, unit, or division supervisors. Such accomplishments only help promote good working relationships between supervisors, subordinates, and others within the agency. Each investigator is a leader based on the responsibility they have assumed within their respective units and expertise. As leaders move into positions of authority, they accept the added responsibility and must never forget how hard they worked to earn their position. Each leader has a crucial role to play during the course of a major crime investigation and they should never abuse their authority. Additionally, real leaders never take credit for the hard work and success that was achieved by others. Leaders gain respect by acknowledging those investigators that successfully closed an investigation, not by putting themselves first. A leader's responsibility, during the course of an investigation, is to monitor, guide, and ensure that each phase of the investigation was completed thoroughly and professionally. In adhering to these basic principles, the team, unit, division, and agency wins. Upon reviewing the accomplishments of the major crime's unit, they reflect positively on the leader at the helm. Therefore, true leaders never have to say how good they are. They just have to point out how successful their team is. The leaders' responsibility is to advance each member of the team and the unit, not themselves. There will come a time when individuals take on the personality of their leader, just make sure that personality is positive and not arrogant or obnoxious. A responsible leader nurtures, mentors, and effectively guides team members in a manner that creates success.

"FEAR AND DOUBT ARE THE CHAINS AND SHACKLES THAT STIFLE AN INVESTIGATOR'S ABILITY TO LEAD." –Cpt. Jose 'Pepi' Granado.

Fighting for Everything

All investigators must fight the good fight and have a base to stand on. As a leader, investigators will come across situations where their decision is not the most popular or expedient. They must be prepared to reason their point with facts and a course of action that will lead to success. An investigator's passion and conviction are the engine that propels the argument forward. The downside is that investigators cannot be so blinded that they fail to observe the pitfalls which can cause them and the investigation to crash and burn. Investigators cannot allow pride to take over.

They must explore every avenue, even if the new path was not set by them. Leaders must resist temptation to fight against fresh ideas and allow for others on the investigative team to actively participate. When leaders incorporate the ideas of those around them, that act fuses the investigative team and creates a bond that lasts well beyond one investigation. Leaders should not be quick to reject others ideas. Leaders should remember that they never climb the ladder of success alone, they had help along the way. An investigator's ability to lead and fight for what is right provides the platform for others to emulate. A leader's legacy as a fighter resonates across all spectrums of the organization they represent and beyond. Leaders that are referred to as 'fighters,' it does not necessarily mean that they are negative or always going against the grain.

Such leaders are willing to put themselves on the line for what they believe in, especially when it comes to defending a position based on facts that will assist in closing a difficult investigation. These fights or differences of opinion mainly occur during the final stages of an investigation, when strategies are being discussed on whether or not to make an arrest based on the evidence and facts. Additionally, some fights occur during the phase when investigators meet with the state attorney who is assigned to the investigation. Mostly, these fights are philosophical based on what approach to take in order to bring the case to trial or what strategy is best served in order to arrest the subject. Fighting for a cause is healthy, so long as you have the facts to articulate your position. Leaders never back down from a good fight and they do not allow for others to dissuade them. As a leader, I always encouraged those investigators under my command to fight for what they believe in and to articulate their point with facts, evidence, and a solution. A leader, during the course of an investigation, must allow other investigators to develop confidence so they can gain the necessary experience which will assist them on future investigations. Investigators cannot use a supervisor as a crutch to avoid responsibility. Remember, the lead investigator has full control of any investigation and team members are assigned to assist, that includes the supervisor.

Sharing Knowledge

Leaders need to know their own strengths, weaknesses, and moral values. Once leaders understand who they are, it makes it easier for them to impart knowledge on to those who want to learn and grow. As a leader, one must be true to the core principles that allows them to properly investigate any major crime without bias. Being straightforward and fair-minded allows for effective leadership. Leaders who have the responsibility of managing a major crime unit must be prepared to mentor those who have less experience. Conversely, supervisors must be ready to mentor and pass on knowledge to the next generation of supervisors without fear of being replaced.

When a young investigator becomes a part of a major crimes team, they do not join the team all knowing. On the contrary, new investigators are barely scratching the surface of investigating a case. It would be unfair for any leader to allow a new, inexperienced investigator to be assigned to investigate a complex incident without knowing the basics. Leaders must take the time to slowly educate the new investigators in order for them to feel comfortable when they respond to a major incident with their team. Leaders must take into account that new investigators will make mistakes along the way. Impress upon the new investigator that mistakes made today lets them build a toolbox of lessons so that these mistakes will not be repeated. Nourishing a young investigator's appetite encourages them to continue asking questions. Leaders should never amputate the spirit of a new investigator. Doing this turns a potential future investigative leader into a nervous performer who just shows up and expects everyone else on the investigative team to carry his weight. The failure of such an investigator falls directly on the leader who oversees the investigative team. A way that good leaders protect their reputation is by teaching *ALL* who wish to learn without advertising. Telling everyone how good you are as a teacher or investigator does not say much about you as a leader. Self-promoting suggests a lack of self-confidence in your ability to lead. Every leader needs to reflect on their accomplishments and failures in order to effectively mentor the next generation of investigators.

Leaders must be passionate about their profession if they are to successfully teach others. Those who are fair-weather leaders are unmasked immediately as deceiving and disingenuous by those they are teaching. Good leaders are innovators willing to go out on a limb in order to get their point across to the new investigator, without fear that they are passing on too much of their knowledge. Leaders need to cast their vision to the new generation of investigators in order to motivate and propel them forward. When mentoring the next generation of investigators, leaders need to inspire and encourage them to believe in themselves. Leaders must paint a positive vision for the new investigator and assure them that not every mistake is earth shattering, so long as it was a mistake of the heart and not the mind.

Informing new investigators that they will encounter fear and uncertainty during their early stages of learning will allow them to face said concerns with resolve. Leaders need to be consistent when mentoring new investigators. They cannot send mixed messages if they want to achieve excellent results. Mixed messages create confusion and might have the new investigator revert back to square one, lacking confidence. Remarkably, excellent teaching creates excellent results and builds excellent teams. As a mentor, standards must be set high to where they seem unattainable. Such high standards ensure that mediocrity is not the standard.

As leaders impart knowledge onto their new investigators, they must reinforce that when conducting an investigation, they are not involved in a race. Investigating a major crime is not about who finishes first, but about who can successfully prosecute the case, no matter how long it takes. Once an investigation starts, it never ends until the offender faces justice. Working in a toxic environment is always an excuse and some organizations are difficult, but in the end, success or failure falls on the lead investigator and the investigative team. Leaders should never blame others for their shortcomings as mentors. Instead, they should be able to teach those around them on how to effectively perform under perceived, undesirable conditions.

Leaders must press upon the new investigators that when the team wins, everyone wins. This can be translated as, once the case has been solved, it is not about the lead investigator's success, but the team's success. Allow your team the flexibility to focus on the bigger picture instead of concentrating on the small frame. Leaders let their team make decisions without fear of being second-guessed. Mentoring is a never-ending job if one wishes to have others succeed. It should be done with passion and without reservations. True leaders and mentors should feel comfort in knowing that their legacies are not found on plaques, but on those that were influenced by your infectious passion for the craft and their success.

Conclusion

In reviewing some of the issues that come into play when dealing with inexperienced investigators and the challenges met by unit leaders, it is easy to see how time plays a huge role in developing future investigative leaders. During the early stages of development, inexperienced investigators are relegated to being a 'go-for' or scribe. These tasks might seem menial, but they play an important role in developing an investigator's character. Inexperienced investigators might be asked to respond to a major crime scene and take charge, a responsibility that must be handled professionally and with confidence, even if experience is lacking. Experienced leaders are charged with instructing new investigators from the moment they are assigned to a team. These initial encounters between leader and subordinate lays the foundation for how a new investigator's career will develop. Experienced investigators are, in and of themselves, leaders, not every lesson falls on the shoulder of the investigative supervisor.

Investigative supervisors have the ability to change or reinforce what an inexperienced investigator has learned from watching and emulating their teammates. It is crucial to understand that during times of *CHAOS*, even inexperienced investigators are looked upon to exude calm and confidence. These traits are principles that can eventually lead any committed investigator toward the path to *LEADERSHIP*.

Effective communication by investigators is paramount in order to proceed with any investigation. Investigators must be clear, direct, and give precise instructions. Instructions that are given cannot be lost in translation. In communicating such instructions, investigators must know the audience to whom they are speaking with. An investigator's attitude on a scene goes a long way in getting things done quickly or reluctantly. Experienced investigators are able to assess the gravity of any situation during the course of investigating a major incident by listening to team members assisting with the investigation. It is important for inexperienced investigators to get in a habit of listening before spewing orders. In getting a good understanding of what is occurring from other team members, instructions are given with a specific purpose. During the course of an investigation, investigators should avoid letting *little* things to become *big* things for no reason. Investigators need to understand that a bad situation can yield a positive outcome if the right choices are employed. Throughout the course of an investigation, investigators must be themselves. They cannot be phonies; they must stay true to their profession and the investigation at hand. People can always detect when an investigator is being disingenuous, an attitude that will always come back to haunt the investigator.

A leader's charisma is infectious and the team usually gravitates to those that display such genuine passion. During the course of a lengthy and difficult investigation, leaders with energy usually galvanize the team in order to achieve a successful conclusion. Every major investigation possesses an enormous amount of challenges that must be confronted and dealt with by the lead investigator. How an investigator (no matter the experience) approaches each challenge will determine the effectiveness of their leadership abilities. Every agency with a major crimes section faces challenges of manpower, inexperience, communication, commitment, and accountability. Successful investigators must be able to overcome such obstacles if they want to effectively lead. A leader's responsibility, during the course of an investigation, is to monitor, guide, and ensure that each phase of the investigation was completed thoroughly and professionally. As a leader assigned to a major crime unit, your rank should not matter. The time that each investigator has dedicated to learning their craft is what gives credence and legitimacy to their perseverance and dedication to investigations being conducted.

As a leader within a specialized unit, investigators will come across situations where their decision is not the most popular or expedient. They must be prepared to reason their point with facts and a course of action that will lead to success. Leaders assigned to a major crime's unit must be prepared to fight the good fight. The downside is that investigators cannot be so blinded that they fail to observe the pitfalls which can cause them and the investigation to crash and burn. Investigators cannot allow pride to take over. Fighting for a cause is healthy, so long as you have the facts to articulate your position. Leaders never back down from a good fight and they do not allow for others to dissuade them without facts to support their position. A leader, during the course of an investigation, must allow other investigators to develop confidence so they can gain the necessary experience which will assist them on future investigations. Micromanaging an investigator by a team leader or supervisor only stifles the growth of the inexperienced investigator. Many supervisors are tempted to make unnecessary corrections on reports based on writing styles. This should never be the rule, example, some people use the word lighting and others use illumination. It is the same word, and supervisors must not become English professors unless the report is horrendously written.

Leaders need to know their own strengths, weaknesses, and moral values. Once leaders understand who they are, it makes it easier for them to impart knowledge onto those who want to learn and grow. A leader's responsibility is to mentor, not do the work for those who are lacking in desire. Nourishing a young investigator's appetite encourages them to continue asking questions. Leaders should never amputate the spirit of a new investigator or one that wishes to learn. A good mentor can always look back at their learning years and appreciate how difficult it was to gain experience and knowledge, especially if no one took the interest to teach them. Remarkably, excellent teaching creates excellent results and builds excellent teams. As a mentor, standards must be set high to where they seem unattainable. Such high standards ensure that mediocrity is not the standard.

This section is not geared toward making senior investigators or lead investigators instant leaders. They should have developed into that role with field experience and a lot of trial and error during their years of being active investigators. Instead, this section is geared toward mentoring the next generation of investigators into becoming engaged and passionate leaders, throughout an investigation and their career. A leader's example goes a long way in the development of an inexperienced investigator. True leaders and mentors should feel comfort in knowing that their legacies are not found on plaques, but on those that were influenced by the infectious passion for the craft and their success. Mentors are always available and should never turn their back on someone willing to learn. Leaders should never fear passing on knowledge. They should embrace the opportunity to make the next generation of investigators better prepared for the ever-changing challenges they will face.

Chapter 7
How to bring the Investigation Together

Investigators Choose

Let us prepare to understand how to bring an investigation together. After reviewing the previous chapters, one should have a general understanding of how an investigation should be conducted. Investigators need to keep in mind that investigations are very fluid and ever changing. Not everything goes as planned or on schedule. The previous chapters serve as guides and a refresher for investigators to avoid cutting corners inadvertently by not following the basic principles of investigatory protocols. Those who endeavor to follow these basic principles and periodically review them should be able to succeed with any assigned investigation. Each chapter gave you an understanding of the principles regarding a major crime investigation within specific areas. These chapters were designed for the inexperienced investigator, as well as the experienced investigator, to understand the reasons why certain procedures are done in the manner in which they were described. These rudimentary procedures were drawn from over thirty years of investigative experience, training, and countless hours of diligently studying both as an investigator and from a supervisor's standpoint. Also, these principles were drawn from multiple cases (studied/investigated) and the best practices that were employed throughout each investigation. *Every step taken is for the purpose of successfully clearing or closing an investigation, even if it does not always work out that way.* Investigators should not be dissuaded from following the basic principles that were outlined. The ultimate goal is to gather as much evidence (physical and verbal) in order to achieve the desired result, but if not, to assist the next investigator who reviews the case file to have a good foundation on which to continue to build.

Inexperienced investigators are geared to go fast, running before they learn to walk. Experienced investigators, at times, become complaisant or indifferent and want to run through an investigation as opposed to walking. Both are grave errors that can affect an investigation's outcome. Therefore, inexperienced investigators must be mentored to be deliberate and methodical, just as experienced investigators must remember their fundamentals of investigations. There is no reason to rush during the course of an investigation. *The investigator's responsibility, regardless of experience, is to the victim and the next of kin.* Throughout this chapter, investigators will be able to follow procedural examples set forth in the previous chapters. Thereby extracting specific areas of importance which can be useful to aspiring investigators during an investigation.

Investigators early in their career knew where they eventually wanted to serve. There are law-enforcement professionals that enjoy working the streets, they have no interest in working cases or the crazy schedules that investigators work. Therefore, once an investigator commits to a specific unit within the criminal investigations section, they should also commit to becoming the very best in their respective field of expertise. Investigators are geared differently; they show a passion and an unwavering commitment to the investigative cause.

Sometimes, they are perceived as arrogant or being better than others, which is totally wrong and opposite from the truth. Investigators are misunderstood because of their tenacity and focus when investigating a violent incident. Non-investigators have the luxury of just showing up on a scene, give a few opinions, suggest a course of action (even if it is unsound), leaving the lead investigator and investigative team hanging by a limb. Something investigators cannot afford to do.

Investigation Begins

The following is how it all begins when one is assigned to a major crime unit, specifically a homicide unit. Here is where the rubber meets the road and the 'clock starts ticking.' These procedures will tie together what was learned in the previous chapters and give a better perspective as to why certain protocols are so important.

Not every notification of a death, homicide, or violent crime will be made at the convenience of the investigator or investigative team. Remember what was discussed in *Mental Preparation*, an investigator might be on their day off, spending time with family, or might have come off shift several hours prior to receiving the call. Investigative teams usually have a 'call-out' schedule and a 'lead' schedule. These schedules allow for investigators to properly prepare for the dreaded call.

Notification of a violent incident usually comes in the form of a direct phone call from the investigative supervisor or through radio communications from any officer on the scene. These officers or supervisors are requesting a homicide investigator to respond to the scene. During a shift, investigators are always monitoring the radio transmissions and can gauge when a response will be needed. In all death cases, a response by a homicide investigator is mandated. If patrol units are dispatched to a violent incident, homicide investigators begin monitoring the situation and receive periodic updates from the violent crime's investigators assigned to the investigation. The on-call homicide investigator continues to monitor until such time when information is established that the incident will not result in a death. On many occasions, homicide investigators respond to render assistance and to guide the violent crimes team if there is a possibility that at some point in time (days, weeks, months, or years), a victim might die as a result of their injuries.

These collaborations are beneficial because it allows both the homicide unit and the violent crimes unit to create a good working relationship. This develops comradery between both units and lets them see how each team works their cases. One advantage to having both units on a scene is that of 'force multiplier' (having additional investigators on a scene). Another reason, information is exchanged firsthand between the investigators and not hours or days later. This puts everyone on the same page, even if the incident is not a homicide.

So, the on-call homicide investigator has just received a call of an incident involving a death, possibly a homicide. Upon receiving this call, the investigator has approximately one hour to respond to the location of the incident. During this hour, the investigator must make contact with the homicide supervisor in order to apprise them of the incident. Most likely, the supervisor was already informed by the communication's supervisor. The homicide supervisor will then assign team members to assist the lead investigator. **Note:** There may be occasions when the on-call team is working their shift and the response time to the incident location is usually fifteen minutes. Additionally, there might be times when the lead investigator is off and a homicide team is working. In such instances, the homicide team working will respond to the scene and begin securing the scene until the lead investigator arrives. There are other factors that come into play, such as, investigators who are scheduled off, weekend call-outs, or manpower shortages due to other investigations. These issues and the allocation of resources falls on the homicide supervisor. An experienced supervisor must be able to manage these situations without any underperformances. But let us dispense from the supervisor's responsibility. Those are the dynamics that fall on a supervisor, not the investigator.

Homicide teams that function at a higher level understand what must be done before the lead investigator arrives on a crime scene. This comes from experience working closely as a 'team.' Additionally, less-experienced homicide teams need guidance from experienced investigators or a seasoned supervisor. Homicide investigations cannot be left in the hands of less-capable investigators or supervisors if success is the goal.

So, all things being equal, the lead investigator is preparing to respond and they have made their notifications via chain of command. Once the lead investigator has made their notifications and receives the names of the investigators that will be assisting with the investigation, they can begin delegating assignments. The most crucial assignment; ensure that the crime scene is totally secured to avoid contamination (*review Crime Scene chapter*). Next, secure all possible witnesses and avoid having them within close proximity to each other (this diminishes the chance of them exchanging information of what they saw or heard). If multiple crime scenes exist, protocols do not change. Follow the steps as if only one crime scene was being worked.

Some investigator's delegate a team member to notify the on-call crime-scene technician, state attorney, and medical examiner, others prefer to make the notifications themselves. The time to make such notifications vary, based on the time of the incident or how much information is readily available. My rule of thumb has always been time of incident. If the incident took place during the week, during working hours when traffic is at its peak, I would make the notifications in order to expedite the on-calls response. If the incident took place in the middle of the night or weekend, I would normally wait until I gathered as much information as possible. This ensured that any questions presented to me could be answered.

All notifications must be noted in the 'Bible' (notepad specific to each investigator). Which investigator made the notifications, times they were done, and who received the calls. Additional information must be noted, such as, which on-call will be responding or not and their estimated time of arrival. This information allows for the investigative team to prepare assignments and begin the initial stage of the investigation.

As the investigative team arrives at the crime scene, the first investigator's responsibility is to ensure that the crime scene is properly secured and to set up a staging area for the investigative team and the various elements that will be assisting. If possible, a mobile command vehicle (M.C.V.) should always be used. This allows for privacy and limits distractions during team briefings, it is also a great place to interview less-crucial witnesses. The M.C.V. is an awesome tool during the course of an investigation, especially during inclement weather. If an M.C.V. is not available, the investigating team must find a staging area that isolates them from distractions (during violent incidents, there are many unnecessary distractions). It is important for the investigating team to have space where they can gather their thoughts, exchange information, make notifications, and set assignments.

Once the investigative team has come together at the designated staging area, the homicide supervisor meets with the lead investigator. This meeting is crucial prior to proceeding with the investigation, it gives the supervisor a sense of how prepared the lead investigator is and what strategies they want to employ. While the team prepares to receive their assignments, supervisors are usually analyzing the initial information regarding the incident. This information is usually received from the operations' supervisor, which details unverified information gathered from the first patrol units who arrived at the scene. Though unverified, the initial information is used by the homicide supervisor to brief the command staff. This briefing allows command staff to prepare for a possible press conference with local media outlets. It also buys the investigative team time to prepare without the continuous interruptions by command-staff personnel wanting to know what is going on.

There is nothing more annoying for an investigator or supervisor who are actively working a violent incident, than to have continuous interruptions by command staff asking the same question, "Anything new?" This badgering slows the process and serves no immediate purpose. Fortunately, these types of occurrences are not so prevalent, especially with larger agencies, but once is once too many.

While in the staging area, the lead investigator and co-lead (if possible) will meet for the first time with the primary officer who will be responsible for writing the initial incident report. During this meeting, the investigators will receive the case number, location of incident, time of dispatch, time of arrival (by police and fire personnel), fire-rescue information, alarm number, and the fire-rescue supervisor that pronounced the victim deceased (on-scene) and the time. Also, if fire rescue transported a victim or victims to local hospitals, what method of transportation was used (ground or air) and the fire-rescue information. Additional information, such as backup officers and their initial responsibilities (scene and witness security, area canvass, scene log) upon arrival at the incident scene is needed. Investigators, at this briefing, will learn if witnesses were identified and secured (by whom), if additional victims (injured or not) exist and their location (secondary scene or hospital).

Additionally, investigators will receive a synopsis of the incident from the primary officer. This preliminary information is crucial in determining where to allocate investigative or patrol resources. *Investigators need to keep in mind that these incidents are fluid and information can change rapidly.* **Note:** Prior to beginning the investigation is not the time to theorize or assume anything. There have been times when non-investigative personnel (Patrol Sgt., Captain, or officers) provide erroneous information without having facts. This can hinder the integrity of the investigative team and the investigation. "One cannot connect the dots, when there are no dots." It always bothered me, when arriving at a violent incident, to hear that a patrol sergeant or others had determined the number of wounds a victim sustained, possible motive or who an offender was based on nothing factual, and provided that information without clearance from the investigative team. All that, just to be relevant. Self-promotion does not give anyone the right to provide wrong information. These individuals should be dissuaded from such behavior. Unfortunately, in many instances they are not.

Once the investigators receive the synopsis from the primary officer, they must meet with the investigative team at the designated staging area or M.C.V. During this crucial meeting, the investigative team will be briefed on what was learned and the course of action which will be employed. Ideally, during this briefing, members of the medical examiner's office (on-call medical examiner), state attorney's office (on-call attorney), and lead crime-scene technician should be present in order to expedite the initial stage of the investigation (there will be times when not all on-call personnel will be present and must be brought up to speed as they arrive). During this session, the lead investigator will inform the investigative team of what was initially learned based on the primary officer's account.

Note: Investigators must ensure that they immortalize in their 'Bible' dates/times of these events, additional events, and what they did, which they can refer to when preparing their supplemental reports pertaining to the investigation.

Upon conclusion of the briefing, each investigator assigned to the investigative team will receive assignments specific to the investigation as dictated by the lead investigator and the team supervisor. Assignments are given based on manpower, experience, and need. Such assignments are, but not limited to, monitoring/supervising and assisting the crime-scene technician in locating, identifying, and collecting evidence (*review Crime Scene chapter*). Other assignments might entail interviewing potential witnesses on scene or in a controlled environment such as the investigative unit's interview room (*review Interview/Interrogation chapter*), responding to the medical facility where some victim/victims (deceased or not) are being treated for their injuries, assisting the on-call medical examiner, and the on-call state attorney.

It is important for investigators to stay focused during investigations that are dynamic in scope. There might be a feeling of being overwhelmed and, sometimes, anxiety takes hold. Investigators need to take a step back, take a deep breath, and follow the steps from A-Z, do not begin to skip steps (this is where investigator's get in trouble and lose control).

Once a plan of action has been outlined and assignments given, the investigative team will conduct a preliminary walkthrough of the crime scene. This walkthrough is crucial on many levels because it gives the lead investigator and the investigative team a close visual of the actual scene. The walkthrough must be conducted carefully as to not contaminate the scene and should be started at a specific point to maintain consistency. Scene notes are crucial and should be documented by the investigator who will be assigned to monitor the on-scene investigation (*review Crime Scene chapter*). These notes should detail evidence such as casings, weapon(s), blood trails, blood spatter, location of victim/victims, strike marks, or any evidence that is observed by a specific investigator. Additionally, drawing the crime scene (not to scale) is beneficial because it allows the lead investigator to reflect on what was observed at the scene when asking future questions of witnesses or offenders. It also helps when the crime-scene report is reviewed, so if any errors are found, they can be corrected. Upon concluding the walkthrough, the investigative team will gather and again brief on what they learned. As the briefing concludes, each investigator will begin assuming their assigned responsibilities. *The lead investigator will then brief their supervisor (who should be on scene), who will in-turn brief the command staff.* It is at this point that the first media release (verbal or written) may be done. There are occasions when media outlets are present and would like a 'sound bite,' it would be the agency's decision if an interview is granted. Nonetheless, at some point, a press release should be submitted. Many times, press releases assist the investigation because of the human-interest aspect.

From this point on, investigative strategies play a big factor on how the lead investigator will proceed with the investigation. Lead investigators normally stay on-scene (on occasions, they do not, based on specific circumstances) and manage the investigation. From this vantage point, they are able to gather needed intelligence that would assist them in conducting future interviews. They might respond to other scenes which includes medical facilities or other crime scenes to gather additional intelligence. If witnesses have been located, lead investigators might certainly respond, for it is the responsibility of the lead investigator to have as much information as possible before conducting any interview. Again, because of the fluidity of the investigation, there might come a point where the lead investigator designates another investigator to conduct specific interviews or respond to specific locations in order to save time. Manpower, during the course of a violent crime investigation, is paramount, and lack thereof limits the effectiveness of the lead investigator and the team. Nonetheless, this is precisely the reason for a lead investigator to allocate resources in a manner that benefits the investigation.

Note: There will be instances when command staff request that an investigator expedite the processing of a scene in order to make the area available for the public to resume regular pedestrian or vehicular traffic. I have heard such requests on many occasions and have needed to respectfully deny said request. The integrity of an investigation is supreme and cannot be circumvented.

At specific points of the investigation, everything that is done by the lead investigator or team must be documented.

While continuing the management of the scene, the lead investigator must coordinate the first canvass of the area where the incident took place. This canvass is pivotal, it allows investigators conducting the canvass to interact with the citizens that reside in the affected area. During this phase, investigators walk the neighborhood, making contact with people on the street, knocking on residential doors (homes or apartments), or entering businesses that are open. Additionally, investigators look for possible evidence such as video-surveillance cameras or physical evidence (strike marks, discarded items related to incident, or even weapons) that was not located during the initial walkthrough of the crime scene. Early canvasses are not always fruitful, citizens may not want to speak with the investigators due to fear of retaliation, but this should not discourage the investigative team. What is important? Those citizens see the investigative team performing their job in a professional manner and not just going through the motions. Remember 'gift of gab,' this is the perfect time for investigators to strike up conversations with people with whom they come in contact. Passing out business cards every chance they get is crucial. This allows people who do not wish to speak at the moment make a call at a later time. It also makes people feel as if they have a direct contact with the police and in some cases, people will call when they come across the investigator's card.

Though the initial canvass might not be successful, that does not mean that it did not have an impact or investigators should stop canvassing the area or speaking to people. Subsequently, all information gathered during the initial canvass must be documented immediately by the investigator who collected it. This ensures strict accountability of what was learned, when, and by whom. After the initial canvass has concluded, the investigative team reconvenes at the staging area or M.C.V. for another briefing. This period is meant for the investigative team to exchange ideas based on what they have learned and to gather their composure before embarking on the next phase. Once the lead investigator has digested what has been presented, they can determine the next course of action. **Note:** At this gathering, all investigators should be updating their 'Bible' based on what they have done. Ideas and information should be exchanged between the investigative team and additional assignments are passed out. If the on-call state attorney or medical examiner are present (sometimes, they are, and sometimes, they are not present), they can take part and hear what has been learned. This helps them prepare their notes for future reports that they must submit.

In the event that search warrants are required, the state attorney will be better prepared, having had first-hand information. As for the medical examiner, they are able to get a sense of why the incident took place and how.

Once the briefing has concluded, the lead investigator or designee will assist the medical examiner during the on-scene physical examination of the decedent (*review M/E chapter*). The lead C.S.I. technician will be present and continue their collection of evidence (photos, G.S.R. swabs, casings, fragments, or clothing) as part of the investigative protocol (*review Crime Scene chapter*). All aspects of the physical examination must be documented by a scribe designated by the lead investigator. Additional information that may lead to a search warrant must be documented, and consultation with the state attorney must be done immediately, before the crime scene is released (*review A.S.A. chapter and Search Warrant examples*).

In many instances, a state attorney is present, and this allows them to have a better sense of the type of investigation that will transpire. It allows them to be better prepared if and when a search warrant is needed, and it gives them a good sense of what to expect when meeting with the lead investigator or witnesses during a pre-file conference (when an arrest is forthcoming or made).

Once the investigative team receives their next assignments, the lead investigator must brief and update their supervisor. This information is crucial in order to update command staff. Team supervisors play a vital role in buffering the investigative team from command staff and public officials who tend to hinder progress (not intentionally) by interjecting and wanting continuous updates. In many cases, updates are provided erroneously by officers or supervisors (who are not involved with the investigation) without verification of the facts. These self-promotions hurt an investigation because on occasions, the information is passed on to media outlets. For this reason, my rule as a supervisor of any investigation was to brief command staff when information was verified (name of victim, gender, and motive) so they could be well informed before being questioned by media. Understand, from an investigative standpoint, information does not always have to be provided right away. There are times when a tactical decision is made to hold off on providing certain information. This is determined on a case-by-case bases.

At this juncture of the investigation, the lead investigator reassesses the security of the crime scene and makes sure that its integrity has not been compromised. Several hours have probably passed and patrol officers become antsy, they want to leave, they are hungry, hot, thirsty, and generally miserable, because they are standing around making sure that no one enters the crime scene. Lead investigators should make it a point to approach officers on these scenes and tell them how vital they are to the investigation, especially if an angry or emotional crowd has gathered outside of the crime scene. These crowds who are agitated tend to put officers on edge, which heightens their awareness and makes them less approachable (a demeanor which may not be taken well by people in the crowd).

Not all crime scenes have large, restless crowds, but the lead investigator must ensure scene integrity. *This means, no one but the investigative team is allowed within the crime scene.*

Once the crime scene has been reevaluated, the physical examination of the victim or victims begins. This process can take some time, depending on the scope of the crime scene (location where victim or victims were discovered and type of injuries sustained). Remember, this part of the investigation is controlled by the medical examiner (they perform an independent investigation based on the victim's physical evidence) who must be meticulous when examining the victim or victims while at the scene. The on-scene physical examination opens the door for what is to be discovered during the postmortem examination which is conducted within a designated period after the victim or victims are removed from the crime scene.

Additionally, investigators who are assigned to assist with the on-scene physical examination have an opportunity to discuss what they have observed with the medical examiner conducting the examination. During these short periods, seasoned medical examiners impart information with the lead investigator based on similar cases in which they assisted with in the past. Investigative notes that are taken by the lead investigator or designee are crucial when preparing the medical examiner's report. These notes are vital for they give a cursory insight as to how the victim or victims were killed. It might depict the type of wounds. **Note:** As previously stated, on-scene physical examinations can take some time and sometimes, are viewed as insensitive because of the need to undress the victim or victims. There are times when these examinations are performed faster (but no less thorough) or because of where the victim or victims are located (inside vehicles, industrial facility, or dwelling), they might be transported directly to the morgue, which is where the physical examination will be performed. These on-scene examinations are sensitive and investigators must take into account that family members may be in the designated area for next of kin. For this reason, all victims and their relatives must be treated with respect and dignity. Family members are desperate for answers, they might be extremely upset and may seem hostile toward investigators. In more cases than not, this anger is not intended toward the investigator. Investigators must remain composed and show empathy to a grieving family. They will thank you later for showing patience. Once the victim or victims are ready to be removed from the crime scene, a medical examiner's report will be prepared by the lead investigator. The medical examiner, prior to leaving, will advise the lead investigator when the postmortem will be performed. Once this is done, the victim-removal team will prepare the victim for removal by wrapping them in a plastic body bag, placing them on a stretcher, and into the van. The lead investigator will then sign custody of the victim or victims to the removal team and give them the medical examiner's report. There will be times when clothing is taken by the removal team for further examination at the morgue. The removal of a victim or victims is delicate, this is when relatives become increasingly emotional and sometimes, might attempt to run into the secured scene. For this reason, I always liked to prepare family members for what was going to happen. (There may be occasions where no N.O.K. are present and notification must be done after.)

Therefore, I would pick out a family member that appeared to be more composed and used them as my point of contact to better control other family members.

Investigators must remember that dealing with family members and emotions is not always easy, but an important responsibility, and if verbal attacks are made, they are not to be taken personally.

Now that the victim or victims were removed from the scene, another briefing must be done by the investigative team. At this point, there is a possibility that not all team members will be present, nonetheless, a briefing with those present is crucial. Members of the investigative team, C.S.I., state attorney, medical examiner (usually never), and command staff (maybe) get an overview of what has been learned to this point in the investigation. Investigators assigned to other tasks will be called to give an update.

As information is compiled, leads that need to be followed up will be assigned, search warrants that must be prepared will be done so by the lead investigator and additional interviews, if necessary, will be assigned. Additionally, specific instructions will be given to the lead crime-scene technician in order to expedite examination of evidence by priority and to have them on standby in the event a search warrant will be executed. Everyone should be updating their 'Bible' while the investigative supervisor is brought up to speed. This is another period for exchange of ideas between the investigative team based on what has been learned. As the investigative team prepares to clear the crime scene, it is the lead investigator's responsibility to meet with the primary officer assigned to prepare the incident report.

During this meeting, the lead investigator will analyze the information the primary officer has for the incident report. This information will be checked for accuracy (many times, reports are prepared and misinformation is entered, such as wrong name for victim or wrong D.O.B. On occasions, a wrong case number is entered along with a wrong location of incident). Although the offense-incident report is the responsibility of the primary officer, it is ultimately the lead investigator's responsibility to ensure total accuracy. Therefore, everything that goes into the report must be approved by the lead investigator, to include the narrative portion (sometimes, officers like to write way too much unnecessary information).

Once the lead investigator has concluded their briefing with the investigative team and primary officer, a final canvass of the crime scene will take place in the event that something was missed. Upon conclusion of this canvass, the lead investigator will give the 'all clear' signal to open the crime scene for pedestrian or vehicular traffic. **Note:** In the event that there are body fluids in an area where people can come in contact with it, the fire department will be requested for a wash down. *Also, keep in mind that a crime scene can be held as long as needed in order to complete an investigation. Once a crime scene has been released, any possible evidence that remained is lost.* Investigators should never be in a rush to release a crime scene; time is on their side. A little inconvenience should not determine when a crime scene is to be released.

Several hours have now passed. The investigative team has cleared the crime scene and they return to their agency. Inside the criminal investigations section, along with crime analysts and victim advocates, another briefing takes place. At this briefing, the investigative team goes over every piece of information that was gathered during the initial stage of the investigation. Historical workups are done in order to ascertain correct data on the victim(s), location where incident took place, witnesses, suspect(s), vehicle(s), and any criminal past or associates of those involved. Additional workups are prepared by the crime analysts, which might include, but not limited to, photographic line-ups, information or probable cause flyers, as well as wanted-for-questioning flyers. These analysts are vital in any investigation and should be used as often as possible. Additionally, the victim's advocates, who are assigned to the investigative team, are given a separate briefing, detailing what took place and a history of the victim(s). With this information, victim advocates make contact with designated family members and inform them if they are able to provide services (funeral expenses, counseling, or temporary shelter) that will assist the next of kin during their time of grief, so long as they meet the criteria.

During this period, while in the station, the investigative team and *ALL* police personnel that did anything regarding the investigation begin to author their individual supplemental reports, independent of each other, depicting what their involvement was. Each supplemental report is reviewed by a supervisor or the lead investigator before they are submitted prior to the end of the shift.

These supplemental reports are extremely helpful to the lead investigator upon reviewing them prior to continuing with the investigation. Lead investigators are not expected to memorialize everything that everyone on a crime scene did, but they are expected to read each officer's or investigator's supplemental report in order to get a better understanding of what was done and who was contacted. If search warrants or arrest warrants are needed, this is when they are prepared, and reviewed by a supervisor, before submitting them to the state attorney assigned to the investigation. Once any warrant is submitted to the state attorney for review, the lead investigator must standby in the event that any corrections are needed. When the corrections are made, the warrant is resubmitted for approval before being presented to the on-call judge. Once the judge signs the warrant, it is now ready to be executed and should be executed expeditiously. (*review Arrest Warrant example*)

In the event that no warrants are being prepared or witnesses being interviewed, the lead investigator will prepare a Majors Memo or 301 Report that will give a synopsis of the event. Either memo will be submitted up the chain of command through channels. A copy will be placed on a homicide clipboard (which is on display in the criminal investigations section) and one will go inside the lead investigator's case file. As the initial phase of the investigation winds down, the lead investigator will brief their supervisor as to what has been done and assignments that are to be completed. Keep in mind, investigations are fluid and they do not always go in a straight line. Investigators must be able to adapt on the fly and move quickly to where leads take them.

Prior to ending their tour of duty and before leaving the station, it is the responsibility of the lead investigator to ensure that *ALL* supplemental reports were submitted, that the homicide board was updated, and new assignments were issued to the investigative team. A final call to the morgue is made in order to obtain the time when the postmortem will be conducted. Once a time has been set, the lead investigator and co-lead will make preparations to attend the postmortem. The rest of the investigative team will respond to a designated location (most likely the crime scene) at the conclusion of the postmortem, if needed. The investigation's complexity will determine how many investigators will be needed or how soon (most times, they are needed the next day). Investigators need to understand that follow-ups are crucial while the iron is hot, but tired and exhausted investigators will slow down any progress. During this period, a seasoned investigator or experienced supervisor can determine the condition of each team member. This will play an important role in order to effectively redeploy them without affecting the investigation.

After a long and hectic start to the investigation, lead investigators and co-leads find themselves at the morgue, preparing to attend the postmortem. On many occasions, a lead investigator and co-lead will attend their victim's postmortem without having slept or rested.

Investigators experience this all the time, they begin a case one day and before they realize, they have been working non-stop for 48 to 72 hours. This is an adrenalin rush that keeps investigators going during an investigation's early stages. Nonetheless, investigators must understand that this pace cannot be sustained without some consequences (short temper, irritability, lack of focus, exhaustion) that can hinder an investigator's ability to function effectively. So, as these investigators attend the postmortem, their team members get some well-needed rest in order to continue with the investigation's mission. Each postmortem is a learning session for any investigator who attends. It allows investigators to get a better understanding of the type of investigation a medical examiner must conduct. Each case is different and presents its own set of issues which can be best explained by the medical examiner who is performing the post-mortem.

Investigators, during the postmortem, are able to see firsthand, the types of injuries that the victim(s) sustained. They will be able to identify wounds and defects associated with the incident and they will be able to observe entrance and exit wounds, as well as trajectory. Questions must be posed to the medical examiner during the postmortem, if not, how can an investigator expand their knowledge of basic anatomy and wound identifications.

As previously documented in the Medical Examiners chapter, investigators must get into a habit of diagraming each wound on the anatomy charts provided to them by the morgue supervisor. In many facilities, anatomical charts are within close proximity to where the postmortem is being performed, so it is accessible to the investigator. **Note:** Investigators need to remember, they will receive a complete autopsy report pertaining to their investigation by the assigned medical examiner. This report is thorough and dimensions are exact, so, in the cursory diagram that was prepared by the investigator, investigators do not need to be exact. They just need to have a general idea of what was learned during the post-mortem examination. Other factors come into play during the postmortem examination, like toxicology or medical history. The results of these areas will not be determined for some time (depending on the laboratory's workload and priority of the case). It could take weeks or months before investigators receive the results. Still, this delay does not preclude the medical examiner from determining the manner or cause of death. A preliminary medical examiner's report will be provided and a notation on this report will state, 'Pending Toxicology'. Investigators must take the opportunity to attend as many postmortem examinations as possible, even if the cases are not theirs. This exposes investigators to an array of cases, many of which they will never investigate. It also gives them familiarity with the doctors who work in the morgue. As investigators gain familiarity with the doctors and investigators that work for the medical examiner's department, they will find how helpful they are when information or reports are needed. Attending postmortem examinations enables investigators to acclimate better to being in close proximity or contact with dead bodies, either on a scene or in the morgue.

Once the investigators conclude their participation in the morgue, the rest of the investigative team is notified (there will be occasions when they will not be needed) and given instructions where to meet. Usually, lead investigators take this opportunity to call and brief the investigative supervisor and state attorney as to what was learned during the postmortem, especially if additional information was gathered. In the event that leads have been received and, depending on the type of leads, it will determine how many investigators from the team will be called to assist with the follow-up. When the investigators leave the morgue, they will most likely return to the initial crime scene. If they respond alone or with additional team members is based on what new intelligence was gathered. *Investigators need to update their 'Bible' or case notes once they leave the morgue, in order to keep a running timeline of what has been done and who did it. This procedure must always be completed before each tour or significant event concludes.*

While the lead investigator is waiting for his team to muster, this is a perfect time for a break, have a meal, contact a family member or significant other. Investigators are on an emotional rollercoaster and they must reconnect with someone or something that grounds them. Investigators are not machines or impervious to emotions, they need space to reenergize themselves.

Once the staging location has been designated, team members will respond expeditiously, prepared to assist with the investigation. The lead investigator has the option of inviting the state attorney assigned to assist, as well as the lead C.S.I. investigator (C.S.I. can wait until they are needed). Lead investigators must impress upon each team member that success of closing the case rests on each investigator's effort, not just the lead investigator. *This gives each team member ownership of the investigation and reduces tardiness to locations and appointments.* Unfortunately, when investigative teams do not mesh in a manner that promotes complete cooperation, they tend to exact minimal effort to the detriment of the investigation and it causes the lead investigator to overextend their efforts. These cases are rare when working with a homicide or violent crime unit because of their professionalism and dedication, but it can happen. In the event it does, this is when a strong supervisor is needed to refocus and redirect the team.

Now that the team and other entities have arrived at the staging area, they will be updated as to what was learned since they last met. Usually, the lead investigator will be the one giving a brief synopsis of the incident (recap) and provide any additional information gathered during the postmortem. This allows each team member to get a full understanding of what took place, type of injuries, and a victimology, in addition to historical facts. Remember, some investigators might not have been present during the on-scene physical examination of the victim or the area canvasses that were conducted initially. This information is necessary in order for the team to be brought up to speed. As each investigator is writing down this information, the lead investigator must begin preparing for the next phase of the investigation.

Upon conclusion of the recap, a lead investigator might want to elicit feedback or suggestions from the team. Again, this promotes unity and gives the lead investigator time to gather their thoughts before assigning new responsibilities.

During this next evolution, team members will again conduct a complete canvass of the immediate area. If necessary, the radius of the area will be extended in an attempt to contact possible witnesses that live outside the initial grid. This canvass might be conducted at an hour different from when the incident took place. This strategy is employed to contact citizens that might have heard something, but were not present or to interview them when they arrive home from work. Upon receiving their new instructions, each team member is responsible for documenting what they do during this phase. Regardless of results, this canvass is probably the most crucial because investigators make contact with citizens, hours after a violent incident has taken place. Making contact with citizens after a violent incident and seeing their reaction allows investigators an opportunity to analyze their demeanor. Citizens' reactions, when they are contacted by an investigator, speaks volumes of how the victim was viewed in the neighborhood or if the victim was a stranger. Engaging these citizens in conversations and letting them speak about the victim (good or bad), what they heard or saw, is vital in piecing together motive, but this task is easier said than done.

If investigators are unable to locate willing and cooperative witnesses during this phase, they should not be discouraged. Business cards or prepared flyers (for public view) must be left with whomever was contacted or at locations which were visited. If businesses are in the area, ask the manager or owner if they would cooperate by posting a flyer. Investigators will find that many businesses will go out of their way to assist law enforcement. This cooperation is cultivated from good police interaction and partnership with businesses in the area. Investigators should also be vigilant for anything that seems out of place that was overlooked during the initial canvass, such as strike marks, discarded evidence, or surveillance cameras. Once the canvass has concluded and if additional witnesses were not located, investigators will return to the staging area for a debriefing. Remember, investigative teams might need to visit and re-canvass a particular location more than once. It could take several canvasses before it bears fruit.

However, if an investigator is able to locate a credible witness or witnesses with vital information, they should not be visibly excited to where others in the area might notice. A witness's safety is paramount and crucial to the investigation. So, they need to be interviewed in such a manner that they feel comfortable and assured that nothing will happen to them for cooperating. Therefore, before any witness is removed from their home or place of business to be interviewed, a game plan must be in place. The method which will be utilized for transporting a crucial witness will be analyzed when the investigating team debriefs.

Investigators must feel confident with how and when a witness will be transported, in order to minimize any future tampering of the witness by nefarious people involved with the violent incident. With the witness's information available to the lead investigator, they can arrange for transportation at a location away from where a witness is living, or they can meet the witness at a predetermined area. These are but a few strategies that can be used, just like setting a specific time for the interview in order to avoid suspicion. Knowing that a witness wants to cooperate is half the battle, getting the witness to cooperate is trickier because many issues can arise to dissuade a cooperating witness (fear, threats, or lack of trust). Therefore, when facing these issues, an investigator must be creative in order to bring about a positive result. In such cases, it is essential for investigators to make a witness feel at ease. Not all witnesses are fidgety, many will cooperate regardless of circumstances simply because they want justice for the victim. Interaction with any witness, for the most part, is simple, it might take some friendly persuading and commitment on the part of the lead investigator besides a reassurance of their safety. Once the logistics have been set, the witness or witnesses are safely transported to the homicide or violent crimes office where they will be properly interviewed and their sworn statements are immortalized.

Understand, this is but a microcosm of how follow-ups during an investigation works. As previously stated, investigations are fluid and many variables come into play. Though many situations seem similar in scope, they are not, but should be used as guides for the next investigation. Investigators must develop a 'mental toolbox' to draw from when needed.

Investigators need to be pliable, willing to adapt, and navigate through rough problems that present themselves during the course of any type investigation. Investigators who create for themselves, what I like to call, the 'tunnel-vision effect,' fail because they are unwilling to make the necessary adjustments. This effect is observed with inexperienced investigators (which can be corrected) or investigators that seem to think they know more than anyone else (this trait is hard to break), though they do not. Such deficiencies can be corrected if the investigators have a desire and willingness to change. Experienced investigators or supervisors play a big role in mentoring these investigators in order to modify their deficiencies.

Now that the follow-up canvass has been completed, the investigative team returns to the staging area and debriefs. Everything that was learned during this phase will be discussed, at which time the lead investigator can determine what course of action to pursue. The next phase is predicated on the leads that are developed or intelligence that is acquired during the interviews of witnesses. Once the debriefing concludes, assignments (if necessary) will be given to assisting investigators. *There will be cases when no leads are developed, then it becomes the lead investigator's responsibility to continue looking under every rock until they have exhausted all efforts.*

These efforts consist of revisiting a victim's family members for additional information, reviewing supplemental reports that were written, listening to the 911 tapes, or listening to witness interviews (if applicable). These are areas which a lead investigator can control. What they cannot control are crucial reports and results from labs or when a citizen decides to call 'crime stoppers' with a tip that can break open the investigation. Lead investigators must always stay creative and develop strategies that will assist in bringing a positive result to the investigation. If a press conference, sketch artist, or polygraph is needed, investigators must make the request. Critical thinking and thinking outside the box is paramount for any investigator, if they wish to succeed. Present each idea to the investigation supervisor or investigation's commander, be rational as to why such a request is being made and for what purpose. Do not ask for a helicopter if one is not needed, fly on your own time.

Note: There will be times during the initial stages of an investigation that a suspect is detained. This does not change the procedures that must be completed, it just changes the timetable for the lead investigator who must now rely on his team without being present. A lead investigator now must focus on how and when to interview the suspect.

With all things being equal, the investigative team has cleared the staging area as the investigation continues. The lead investigator must brief their supervisor so they can brief the command staff. While the investigative team is in the homicide office, they are updating their 'Bibles,' meeting with the lead crime-scene technician, and keeping the state attorney informed on the progress being made.

The lead investigator will assign members of his team to attend every 'roll call' and brief patrol units as to what took place and how they can assist with the investigation. Meetings will then be scheduled (within 24 hours of incident) with specialized units such as gangs, narcotics, crime suppression, or community-policing teams in order to use them in a supporting role (remember thinking outside the box). These units perform specific functions that can assist the lead investigator by obtaining leads, witnesses, and possibly a suspect's information. As a force multiplier, these units complement the investigative team by adding anywhere from six to ten investigators at any given time. Investigators must keep in mind that these units are under their command for a specific investigation and anything they do must first be approved by the lead investigator or supervisor. Investigators must caution *ALL* support units and their supervisors that conducting any parallel investigation pertaining to a specific investigation is strictly prohibited and counterproductive.

Administrative responsibilities must be maintained by the lead investigator at all times. Lead investigators must ensure that any documents or reports have been completed in a timely manner and submitted for review, regardless of who is preparing the documents. *The lead investigator is responsible for their investigation; therefore, they must not expect or rely on others turning in documents expeditiously.*

That is why, during down times, they must make sure that all documents have been prepared and submitted by investigators assisting with the investigation. Additionally, this is when the investigation's case file needs to be started by the lead investigator. Investigators should never wait until the last minute to begin setting up their case file. Documents pertaining to any investigation must be placed and secured in each case file immediately upon being received. This ensures accountability as the investigation progresses. There are specific ways of setting up a case file, this allows investigators to retrieve particular documents without disturbing the remaining documents. **Note:** At the end of this chapter, there will be a template to show how a case file should be organized to maximize efficiency. A good habit to follow is to prepare a second case file (*NO ORIGINAL DOCUMENTS*) for the state attorney assigned to the investigation.

Within the first 72 hours, many factors come into play which will dictate as to how an investigation will progress. If witnesses have been identified and located, they must be transported (voluntarily) to the criminal investigations section immediately to be formally interviewed regarding their knowledge of the incident in question. Investigators cannot afford to procrastinate with respects to interviewing witnesses, especially if the witness observed the incident. The longer an investigator takes to interview key witnesses, the further behind they fall with respects to solving the case. Investigators must be dedicated to a fault when it comes to their cases. They need to understand that time is on the offender's side if leads are not immediately followed up. Therefore, the notion of taking time off while conducting any investigation while leads are fresh is unacceptable and a detriment to the investigation.

Let us assume that a witness was transported voluntarily to the criminal investigations section. They were formally interviewed by the lead investigator, provided a sworn statement, and positively identified the offender (must be done in a manner that cannot be contested) because they personally know them or picked them out of a line-up. An event such as this can occur in a heartbeat and when it is least expected. Investigators do not have the luxury of 'wait until tomorrow.' They must continue and fight through exhaustion that is why they are part of a team. Investigators need to remember, this is not a television show and investigations are not always solved in an hour. Therefore, investigators must be prepared for bumps on the road and not become overly excited one way or another. They must maintain a calm, cool demeanor and navigate through any obstacle which can present itself. Anything, from the subject having fled the city or state where the incident occurred to not finding the state attorney in order to review an arrest warrant.

IN THE CIRCUIT COURT OF THE ELEVENTH JUDICIAL CIRCUIT
IN AND FOR MIAMI-DADE COUNTY, FLORIDA

STATE OF FLORIDA)

SS|

COUNTY OF MIAMI-DADE)

STATEMENT OF FACTS SUPPORTING ARREST WARRANT

Before me, ______________________, a judge of the Circuit Court of the Eleventh Judicial Circuit in and for Miami-Dade County, Florida, Personally appeared Detective Full Name of the City of Agency Police Department, Homicide Unit, badge # ; who being by me first duly sworn, deposes and says that he has probable cause to arrest Subjects Name aka "Desolation" (hereinafter referred to as "Offender 1") with a date of birth of Month/Day, 1990 for violation of Florida Statute §782.04 felony first degree murder and armed robbery with a firearm.

Your Affiant's reasons for the belief that he has probable cause to effectuate such arrest are as follows:

Your Affiant has been employed as a law enforcement officer in the State of Florida for 35 years, including 25 years as a homicide investigator at the Agency Police Department. Your Affiant has been employed by the Agency Police Department for the last 10 years. Your Affiant has investigated dozens of homicides in the jurisdiction of City, Name of County State. He has also been assigned the investigation in the homicide of Victim's Name DOB Month/Day, 1994 (hereinafter "The Victim" or "victim") who was discovered deceased on Day/ Date, 2016 at 6:08 am. This incident is being investigated under Agency Police Department case number 2016-XXXXXXX.

On Day/Date, 2016 at 0608 am, Agency Police Department emergency services responded to Green View Park, located at 11111 NW 11th Avenue, City, State/Zip Code regarding the discovery of a deceased black male. The preliminary investigation revealed that the victim had sustained numerous apparent gunshot wounds. The victim was observed wearing a T-

ASA Initials_____
Affiant's Initials_____
Judge's Initials_____

shirt and underwear. At the time of his discovery the victim had no personal possessions, cellular telephone or vehicle.

Your Affiant learned from Agency Police Detective Full Name that on Day, Date, 2016 at 9:09 pm he spoke with relatives of the victim who informed him that the victim left his residence to meet with an unidentified female. The relatives also advised that the victim had in his possession a cellphone and was driving a 2010 Make/Model, light blue in color with a State license plate number of XXXXXX. The registered owner to his vehicle was the victim's sister Full Name who reported the vehicle stolen, to the City Agency Police Department case number 2016-XXXXXX. Additionally, the victim's relatives provided the police with a screenshot photograph of the unknown female the victim was going to meet. The photograph depicted a young Type female with a distinctive tattoo on her chest.

Your Affiant on Day, Date, 2016 attended the autopsy of the victim which was performed at the Name of County Medical Examiner's facility. The postmortem examination was conducted by Associate Medical Examiner Dr. Full Name who determined that the cause of the victim's death was due to multiple gunshot wounds and the manner of death was homicide. The Medical Examiner's case number was noted to be 2016-XXXX.

Your Affiant also learned that on Day, Date, 2016 at 4:05 pm an automated license plate reader (LPR) alerted to the victim's stolen vehicle in the area of NW 111th Street. The Agency Police Department personnel canvass the area and located the stolen vehicle parked unoccupied in the area of NW 112th Street and surveillance was established of the vehicle.

Your Affiant learned that at 5:48 pm a black male was observed walking toward the stolen vehicle and entered the vehicle. Agency police officers attempted to apprehend the black male who accelerated the vehicle and fled the area. A vehicle pursuit ensued. The stolen vehicle stopped at a dead-end street on the next block and the lone occupant fled on foot from the vehicle.

Your Affiant further learned that at 6:00 pm the black male occupant of the stolen vehicle was apprehended at 11111 NW 17th Avenue by Agency police officers. He was identified as Full Name DOB Date, 1993. He was transported from the place of his arrest to be interviewed by Agency Police Department Criminal Investigation Section.

ASA Initials ______
Affiant's Initials______
Judge's Initials______

Your Affiant learned that a black female resident of the townhouse located at 22222 NW 19th Street was identified as the unknown black female with the distinctive tattoo in the photograph provided to the police by the victim's family. She was identified as Full Name DOB Date, 1994. She was transported to the Agency Police Department Criminal Investigation Section.

Your Affiant conducted a recorded interview of Ms. Full Name wherein she identified the screenshot photograph provided by the victim's family as being her. Additionally, she identified a photograph the victim as the man she had text and telephone contact with and who she met on Day, Date, 2016. Additionally, during the interview of Full Name she advised that she was requested by a black male known to her as Rampage to entice the victim to the park so that he could rob the victim and she complied.

Your Affiant learned from Ms. Full Name that she was in telephone contact with the victim and provided him directions to her location. Further she advised that the victim transported her to a nearby park where they subsequently exited his vehicle and sat in the playground area of the park. Additionally, she advised that the black male known to her as Rampage approach them armed with a handgun and demanded property. Also, she advised that Rampage told her to pull the victims pants down and as she complied.

Your Affiant also learned from Ms. Full Name that while she was removing the victims pants the victim ran away and that she also ran away in the opposite direction. Further she advised that while running away she heard multiple gunshots.

Your Affiant also conducted the recorded interview of Mr. Full Name who was arrested for being in possession of the victim's stolen vehicle. He related that during the early morning hours of Day, Date, 2016 he was at the Name of residence located at 11111 NW 19th, Avenue when a black male known to him as Full Name a.k.a. "Desolation", woke him up and informed him that he was going to do a robbery. Furthermore Mr. Full Name related that later that day Full Name a.k.a. "Desolation" admitted to him that he had shot a man in the butt at the park. In addition, Mr. Full Name advised that from Day, Date, 2016 through Day, Date, 2016 Full Name a.k.a. "Desolation" was in possession of a light blue Make automobile which he Mr. Full Name had also occupied earlier that Day.

Your Affiant completed a photographic lineup containing the photograph of Full Name a.k.a. "Desolation" along with the photograph of five (5) other black males which was shown to

ASA Initials _____
Affiant's Initials_____
Judge's Initials_____

Mr. Full Name. He identified the photograph of Full Name in position number three (3) as the man he knows as "Desolation" who admitted to him that he had shot a man in the park.

Your Affiant completed a separate photographic lineup containing the photograph of Full Name a.k.a. "Desolation" along with the photograph of five (5) other black males which was shown to Ms. Full Name. She identified the photograph of Full Name in position number two (2) as the man she knows as "Desolation" who enlisted her aid in conducting the robbery of the victim and who she witnessed in possession of a firearm during the robbery of the victim.

WHEREFORE, for the foregoing reasons, "Your Affiant" requests a warrant for the arrest of Full Name a.k.a "Desolation", with a date of birth of Date, 1990 for violation of Florida Statute §782.04 felony first degree murder and armed robbery of Full Name based on the probable cause herein shown.

____
AFFIANT
Detective Full Name
City of Agency Police Department

SWORN TO AND SUBSCRIBED before me this _______ day of _______, 2016.

____
JUDGE OF THE CIRCUIT COURT
OF THE ELEVENTH JUDICIAL
CIRCUIT OF FLORIDA

ASA Initials ______
Affiant's Initials ______
Judge's Initials ______

These are but a few of the things that can happen and investigators must stay composed.

Understanding that all investigations are fluid, let us consider that the offender is not aware that they were positively identified. Investigators need to slow it down, rushing at this point is a recipe for errors. Now, time is on the investigator's side.

Investigators must notify the state attorney assigned to the investigation and brief them in detail as to what was learned. They should inform the state attorney that the witness is present and prepared to attend a pre-file conference (this is when an assistant state attorney meets with a witness in order to formally interview them before going forward with a case). This procedure might differ in other states or jurisdictions, but in Florida, especially Miami-Dade County, this practice ensures that no missteps are taken by the investigator prior to making an arrest. This is when a good relationship between the state attorney's office, investigating agency, and particularly the investigator conducting the investigation, becomes crucial. If, at any point, trust comes into question, the investigation will suffer because of an overzealous investigator. There is a reason why investigations must be conducted slowly and methodically. The likelihood of mistakes diminishes.

Once the lead investigator meets with the assistant state attorney assigned to the investigation, they present their statement of facts along with any and all evidence to support the statement of facts. This information, along with the investigator's accounts of the investigation, is reviewed by the assistant state attorney. The findings and facts will determine if the assistant state attorney will authorize proceeding with an arrest or if there is enough for an arrest warrant. Additionally, search warrants will be discussed based on any nexus which directly connects the offender with some particular location or electronics that a lead investigator deems necessary to search. When the pre-file conference concludes, any and all witnesses are transported to a location (usually their home) where they can be located at a later date (this can fluctuate depending on who the witnesses are).

The lead investigator must return to the criminal investigations section to prepare the arrest warrant or search warrant if required (upon arrival, the investigation's supervisor should be briefed). Take into account that whoever authors either warrant becomes an affiant to the facts. There will be times when a designated investigator, (co-lead) who is assisting with an investigation, will prepare a search warrant. The arrest warrant is usually reserved for the lead investigator. While these warrants are being prepared, other team members assist by setting up on locations where the offender might be hiding or ensuring that a location where a search warrant will be served is secured. **Note:** For the purpose of the arrest warrant, most likely a probable-cause flyer has been issued. Therefore, any investigative team that locates the offender can apprehend them and transport them to the investigations section for questioning. If not located immediately, the arrest warrant, once it has been signed by a judge, will be entered into the system (N.C.I.C./F.C.I.C.) to where any officer that comes in contact with them can execute the arrest. Depending where the offender was apprehended will determine what steps must be taken by the lead investigator. If an offender is apprehended out of the city, county, or state where the incident took place, the lead investigator and co-lead must travel to where the apprehension took place in an attempt to interview them. Extradition considerations must be weighed when an offender is apprehended outside of the incident's jurisdiction.

As for the search warrant, if the offender was apprehended at a location where evidence might be located, that location must be secured until a search warrant is executed.

Investigators need to understand that an investigation's dynamics can go from 0-100 mph in a matter of minutes. Therefore, investigators must stay mentally strong. In recapping key points of what has developed since the violent incident took place, the lead investigator was assigned as the lead, managed the crime scene, attended the postmortem, performed their administrative responsibilities, located and interviewed a witness or witnesses, met with the assistant state attorney assigned to the investigation, and prepared an arrest warrant and a search warrant. These events could have taken one day, four days, months or years, evidence will determine how long it will take to achieve these steps.

**IN THE CIRCUIT COURT OF THE ELEVENTH JUDICIAL CIRCUIT
IN AND FOR MIAMI-DADE COUNTY, FLORIDA**

STATE OF FLORIDA)
) SS
COUNTY OF MIAMI-DADE)

AFFIDAVIT FOR SEARCH WARRANT

Before me, ____, a Judge of the Circuit Court of the Eleventh Judicial Circuit of Florida, electronically appeared Detective Full Name, Court Identification Number #8, City of Agency Police Department, who being sworn in by ____, deposes and says that he has probable cause to believe and does believe that evidence of a crime is located at the below described premises, which is located in the city of **Name**, in **Name** of County, State, and hereinafter referred to as the "Vehicle."

DESCRIPTION OF THE VEHICLE TO BE SEARCHED

The vehicle to be searched is a 2008, 4door, White, Make/Model, VIN# xxxxxxxxxxxxxxxxx, located at **Tow Company**, XXXX W XXrd Ave, **City**, **Name of County**, **State** Zip Code.

STATUTE(S) BEING VIOLATED

Florida Statute § 782.04 Murder

PROPERTY SOUGHT

Your Affiant seeks to search "The Vehicle" described above and to seize the below-described evidence, with the proper and necessary assistance of civilians, and further, to conduct a forensic examination of any of the listed items, if necessary:

1. Any and all items used to commit or aid in the commission of a Murder, including firearms, ammunition, projectiles, casings and or gunshot residue. As defined by Florida Statute

Affiant's Initials _______ Page 1 Judge's Initials _______

§ 790.001(6), "Firearm" means any weapon (including a starter gun) which will, is designed to, or may readily be converted to expel a projectile by the action of an explosive; the frame or receiver of any such weapon; any firearm muffler or firearm silencer; any destructive device; or any machine gun.

2. Any and all evidence that would lead to the identification of the person(s) responsible for the Murder, including but not limited to, items of forensic and/or investigative significance fingerprints, including blood and/or hair and/or other serological evidence, items useful in identifying recent occupants.

3. Any and all evidence that would lead to the identification of the person(s) responsible for the Murder, including but not limited to, identification documents, drivers' licenses, receipts, and/or bills.

4. All of which items detailed in paragraphs one (1), two (2), and three (3) above are hereinafter referred to as "The Property."

GROUNDS FOR ISSUANCE

Evidence relevant to proving a felony has been committed is contained therein. The facts establishing the grounds for this affidavit and the probable cause for believing that such facts exist are detailed below.

PROBABLE CAUSE

Your Affiant is Detective Full Name, Court Identification Number # of the Agency Police Department. Your Affiant has been a police officer for twenty-three (23) years and is currently assigned to the Agency Police Department Homicide Unit. "Your Affiant" is currently the lead Detective assigned to Agency Police Department case number #2018-XXXXXX, the Murder of Full Name (W/M; DOB: 00/00/1997), hereinafter referred to as the "Victim", which occurred on Sunday, Month 27, 2018.

This affidavit is based upon information known personally to "Your Affiant" based upon investigation and information obtained from others who have investigated this matter and/or have personal knowledge of the facts herein. Because this affidavit is being submitted for a limited purpose of establishing probable cause, your affiant has not included every aspect, fact, or detail of this investigation.

On Sunday, Month 27, 2018, your affiant was assigned to conduct a follow-up investigation regarding the facts and circumstances involving the Homicide of the "Victim", reported under case number #2018-XXXXXX. During the course of the investigation, your Affiant has learned the following:

On Sunday, Month 27, 2018 at 12:55 pm, members of the Agency Police Department responded to XXXXX NW XXth Ave, City, Name of County, State Zip Code in reference to a person shot. Officers responded to the area of NW XXXth St and NW XXth Ave and located a white male, laid on the grass in front of the "Vehicle" northwest from the intersection of NW XXXth St and NW XXth Ave suffering from apparent gunshot wounds.

Designated Fire Rescue #, under the direction of Lt. Full Name responded and pronounced the "Victim" deceased on scene at 1:06 pm, Alarm #1111111.

Interviews with witnesses indicated they heard what they believed to be a transformer exploding and looked outside to see the "Victim" on the ground and a silver vehicle departing the scene.

An inquiry of the "Vehicle's" State vehicle license plate reveled the "Vehicle" was registered to Full Name, XXXXX NW XXth Ct, City, Name of County, State Zip Code. Agency Police Department personnel responded to the location upon request of the Agency Police Department. Contact with the registered owners revealed the "Vehicle" was in possession of their son, the "Victim" whose identity was later confirmed through a driver's license photograph.

"Your Affiant" responded and spoke with Full Name. "Your Affiant" was informed the "Victim" was at home and departed the residence at approximately 12:00 pm. "Your Affiant" was also told prior to departing the residence, the "Victim" stated he couldn't believe that his friends would burglarize his residence, referring to a burglary that occurred approximately five months prior.

On Monday, Month 28, 2018, an autopsy was performed of the "Victim" by Dr. Full Name of the County Medical Examiner's Office. Dr. Full Name ruled the cause of death to be a gunshot and deemed the manner of death a homicide.

On Tuesday, Month 29, 2018, "Your Affiant" obtained video surveillance footage showing the "Victim" arriving at the incident location in the "Vehicle." The footage shows the "Victim" exiting the "Vehicle" and removes items from the trunk area and entered into another vehicle which arrived on scene. As the "Victim" exited the suspect vehicle; no longer in possession of the items carried to the suspect vehicle; two muzzle flashes are observed and the "Victim" is seen falling to the ground. The suspect vehicle is observed stopping near the "Victim", an individual exits the vehicle and approaches the "Victim." The suspect vehicle is then observed driving eastbound on NW XXXth St.

Due to the "Victim" being found deceased in front of the "Vehicle", confirmation the "Vehicle" was operated by the "Victim" and surveillance footage showing the "Victim" removing items from the "Vehicle", it is believed that based upon the foregoing, there is probable cause to believe that the items described above as "The Property" are located in "The Vehicle."

WHEREFORE, Your Affiant prays that a Search Warrant be issued commanding the Chief of Police of the Agency Police Department, or any of his duly constituted agents or officers, the Director of the Agency Police Department, who is also known as the Sheriff of Name County, Florida, or his

Deputies, and the Commissioner of the State Department of Law Enforcement, or any of his duly constituted agents, and all Investigators of the State Attorney of the Designated Judicial Circuit of State, all with the proper and necessary assistance, to search "The Vehicle" above-described, and all spaces therein, for "The Property" above-described, making the search in the Daytime or the Nighttime, as the exigencies may demand or require, or on Sunday, and if the same be found on "The Vehicle" to seize the same as evidence.

____
Detective Full Name
Agency Police Department
ID #(Agency #)
AFFIANT

SWORN TO AND SUBSCRIBED before me this the ________________________ day of ______________________________, ___________.

____

NAME: ________________________________

TITLE: ________________________________

AGENCY: ______________________________

COURT ID: ______________________________

IN THE CIRCUIT COURT OF THE ELEVENTH JUDICIAL CIRCUIT
IN AND FOR MIAMI-DADE COUNTY, FLORIDA

Affiant's Initials ______ Page 5 Judge's Initials ______

STATE OF FLORIDA)
) SS
COUNTY OF MIAMI-DADE)

SEARCH WARRANT

IN THE NAME OF THE STATE OF FLORIDA, TO ALL AND SINGULAR:

The Chief of Police of the Agency Police Department, or any of his duly constituted agents or officers, and the Director of the Agency Police Department, Name of County, State, who is also known as the Sheriff of Name of County, State, or his Deputies, and the Commissioner of the State Department of Law Enforcement, or any of his duly constituted Agents, and all Investigators of the State Attorney of the Designated Judicial Circuit of State, Name of County, State, with proper and necessary assistance.

Affidavit having been made by Detective Full Name of the Agency Police Department Identification Number #, a Homicide Investigator with the City of Agency Police Department Homicide Unit, who being first duly sworn by ______________________________, deposes and says that he has probable cause to believe and does believe that the property constitutes evidence relevant to proving that a felony has been committed, at the below described premises, which is located at the Agency's Police Department, which is located in the City of Name in Name of County, State, and hereinafter referred to as "The Vehicle"

DESCRIPTION OF THE VEHICLE TO BE SEARCHED

The vehicle to be searched is a 2008, 4door, White, Make & Model, VIN# XXXXXXXXXXXXXXXXX, located at Tow Company, XXXX W XXnd Ave, City, Name of County, State & Zip Code.

STATUTE(S) BEING VIOLATED

Florida Statute § 782.04 Murder

GROUNDS FOR ISSUANCE

The facts upon which the Affiant's belief is based have been stated under oath and are set out

Affiant's Initials _______ Page 6 Judge's Initials _______

in the Affiant's AFFIDAVIT FOR SEARCH WARRANT. These facts are now incorporated herein and made a part of this SEARCH WARRANT.

NOW THEREFORE, the facts upon which the belief of said Affiant is based as set out in said AFFIDAVIT FOR SEARCH WARRANT are hereby deemed sufficient to show probable cause for the issuance of a Search Warrant in accordance with the application of the Affiant. And as I am satisfied that there is probable cause to believe that "The Vehicle" described below contains articles of evidence inside and I find probable cause for the issuance of this Search Warrant.

PROPERTY SOUGHT

This Court authorizes the officers, agents and investigators of the above referenced agencies to search "The Vehicle" described above and seize the below-described evidence with the proper and necessary assistance of civilians, and further, to conduct a forensic examination of any of the listed items, if necessary:

1. Any and all items used to commit or aid in the commission of a Murder, including firearms, ammunition, projectiles, casings and or gunshot residue. As defined by Florida Statute § 790.001(6), "Firearm" means any weapon (including a starter gun) which will, is designed to, or may readily be converted to expel a projectile by the action of an explosive; the frame or receiver of any such weapon; any firearm muffler or firearm silencer; any destructive device; or any machine gun.

2. Any and all evidence that would lead to the identification of the person(s) responsible for the Murder, including but not limited to, items of forensic and/or investigative significance fingerprints, including blood and/or hair and/or other serological evidence, items useful in identifying recent occupants.

3. Any and all evidence that would lead to the identification of the person(s) responsible for the Murder, including but not limited to, identification documents, drivers' licenses, receipts, and/or bills.

4. All of which items detailed in paragraphs one (1), two (2), and three (3) above are hereinafter referred to as "The Property."

YOU ARE HEREBY COMMANDED to enter and search "The Vehicle" for "The Property" above-described, and all spaces therein, for "The Property" above-described, serving this warrant and making the search in the Daytime or the Nighttime, as the exigencies may demand or require, or on Sunday, with the proper and necessary assistance, within ten (10) days from the date of issuance and if "The Property" above-described be found there, to seize the same evidence and to arrest all persons in the unlawful possession thereof, leaving a copy of this Warrant and a receipt for the property taken and prepare a written inventory of the property seized and return this Warrant before a court having competent jurisdiction of the offense within ten (10) days from the date of execution as required by law.

WITNESS MY HAND and seal this the ______________________ day of ____________________________, ________.

____
JUDGE OF THE CIRCUIT COURT OF THE
ELEVENTH JUDICIAL CIRCUIT OF FLORIDA

STATE OF FLORIDA)
) SS
COUNTY OF MIAMI-DADE)

RETURN AND INVENTORY

I, ______________________________, received the attached Search Warrant on ______________________________, ________, and duly executed it as follows:

On ____________________, __________, at ______ o'clock ___M., I searched the (premises) (motor vehicle) described in the Search Warrant and left a copy of the Search Warrant with: ______________________________, together with an inventory of property taken pursuant to the Search Warrant:

(USE REVERSE SIDE FOR CONTINUATION)

I, ______________________________, the officer by whom the warrant was executed, do swear that the above Inventory contains a true and detailed account of all the property taken by me on said Warrant.

____

Knowing that there is no set time for when an investigation will conclude, why rush. Investigators must keep that in their head, there is no need to rush. Now that a search warrant has been authored, approved by the assistant state attorney, and signed by a judge, it is the lead investigator's responsibility to execute the search warrant. Whether the search warrant is for a vehicle, dwelling, electronics or other type structure, crime scene protocols must be followed.

The basic procedure when executing a search warrant should not be made any harder than it needs to be. Investigators have a responsibility to their investigation, but they must remain cognizant of the people who are temporarily displaced while the search warrant is being executed. Human nature limits the patience of people who are waiting outside their home or business owners who must close their business while investigators perform their duty. Lead investigators should take the time to explain the process, even if the people do not want to listen.

With that in mind, the investigation has led investigators to a point where a search warrant was authorized based on the facts. With the search warrant in hand, lead investigators should be in contact with the investigators who have secured the location that will be searched. Once communication is made, inform them of an approximate time of arrival and brief the investigative supervisor of what will take place. Additionally, contact the lead C.S.I. technician and inform them that their presence is required at the location in order to document and collect any evidence found that is associated with the investigation. Once notifications have been made to pertinent individuals involved with the investigation, advise them where they should stage to be briefed. During this briefing, the lead investigator will instruct those who are present of their assignments and responsibilities. Any additional information will be forwarded on a need-to-know basis, this is to eliminate anyone outside of the investigative team to have access, which could be unintentionally divulged.

Prior to executing the search warrant, it is the lead investigator's responsibility to have a lieutenant or above present. It is preferred to have an investigation's lieutenant or captain available for the purpose of consistency, if not, any on-duty command-staff personnel will suffice. The lead investigator will inform the primary resident or business owner of what is taking place and present them with the search warrant. In the event no one is present, the same procedure is executed, except that a copy of the search warrant is left inside the location. Before entry is made, the C.S.I. technician will photograph the search warrant, location being served, to depict the address and condition of the entry point. If a door must be forcefully breached, any and all damage will be documented. Once entry is made by the investigative team, the location's interior is searched for officer safety. Nothing is to be disturbed, everything is to stay in place until the clear signal is given. Once it is safe to proceed, the lead C.S.I. technician should be the first to make entry along with the lead investigator. At this stage, the C.S.I. technician should be documenting the interior through photographs or video, and specific items located by the lead investigator should be focused on. While the C.S.I. technician is photographing, the lead investigator or designated scribe should be taking notes of the interior (not to scale) in order to have a good idea of the location's layout, as well as where items were visible. This process can take time depending on how large or disturbed the area might be.

Once the C.S.I. technician has completed photographing and the interior has been documented, this is when the investigative team can enter to begin searching for evidence pertaining to the investigation. This phase must be performed in a methodical and deliberate manner. Investigators will be assigned specific areas of responsibility within the search location. They will document the assigned area (N.E. bedroom, closet in N wall, etc.), what was observed, searched, and if anything was located. Investigators should make every effort not to destroy property or to make a bigger mess than necessary.

In the event that items of evidentiary value are located, investigators must stop, notify the lead investigator (who will document the find) and C.S.I. technician (who will photograph and collect the evidence). There may be instances where more than one piece of evidence is located, that does not change the method of documentation and collection. It is important for lead investigators to be consistent with their investigations and procedures, this limits errors. Additionally, if ever questioned under oath whether or not a particular search warrant, during an investigation, differed from another, it would be easy for any investigator to explain that all protocols and procedures are strictly followed and change only occurs based on specific circumstances which can be explained. Documentation of a location when a search is being conducted is tedious work, everything that is done and who did it must be written down for future reports and they must match with the specific investigator's notes. Upon completion of the initial search, the investigative team will debrief and review what evidence was found (if any).

Investigators now must make a determination if the location being searched will be released to the residents or business owners. This is an important moment because once the location is released to the proper individual, it cannot be searched again without another search warrant. Therefore, lead investigators should get in a habit of reviewing what was learned during a search, re-interviewing witnesses (if applicable), confer with the state attorney assigned to the investigation, and perform a secondary search in order to ensure that nothing was missed. Once an investigator is satisfied with the outcome, then the location can be released.

Note: Lead investigators need to document everything that was collected on an inventory sheet, leaving a copy with the residents or business owner. If the location is empty, leave the inventory sheet inside prior to securing and leaving the location. The clerk of court must receive the return of inventory within 10 days of the search warrant being executed. Investigators cannot procrastinate, this must be done within the specific timeframe. It has always been my practice to get a search warrant for any search needed in furtherance of a violent incident investigation. There may be circumstances where a consent to search can be acquired, but for the purpose of a major investigation, there is no reason to take a chance of a search being contested. Remember what I said about consistency? I can attest that over 90% of major investigations that I supervised or investigated; a search warrant was obtained. Now, it is up to individual investigative teams to determine what works for them. This is not to say a consent to search is not acceptable, but just think about crucial evidence which can be dismissed if a search is deemed illegal or coerced.

Things have been working out and the investigation is moving along. Once the lead investigator and their team leave the search location, they should return to their office in order to debrief. This debriefing is crucial because everything that was learned gets discussed and adds pieces to the investigation's puzzle. Evidence that was located is examined for its value, and consultation with the C.S.I. technician is done to weigh how best to proceed with processing the evidence. If evidence like cellphones or computers are confiscated, search warrants will be needed for each. Therefore, consultation with the assistant state attorney assigned to the investigation is recommended. With laws governing cybercrimes, assistant state attorneys assigned to the cybercrime's unit should be used. **Note:** This is a perfect time for the lead investigator to thoroughly brief their supervisor. Granted, the investigation's supervisor has been actively assisting, but since they are not micromanaging, a lead investigator should be constantly communicating with them on all aspects of the investigation.

As the investigation continues, there will be instances when a possible subject has been interviewed, but there is not enough physical evidence to justify an arrest, baring the subject confessing. It would be prudent at this point, to release the subject. With items such as cellphones or computers in hand, investigators must continue with the forensic autopsy of the investigation. This will either clear a suspect or provide evidence to arrest a subject. Remember, one is seeking the truth and if exculpatory evidence is discovered, that is part of the investigation.

If a suspect was interviewed and they provided information, it would be prudent for the lead investigator to follow-up on what they learned during the interview. An investigator's responsibility is to follow the leads to where they take them, not to tailor information to fit the crime. Facts that are uncovered during the course of any investigation should coincide with the evidence, both physical and verbal, that was collected. These factors play a large role before determining if there is enough evidence to arrest and successfully prosecute an offender. Additionally, they play a larger role in clearing any suspect of culpability. So, based on the developments uncovered during the search, it would make sense to wait for the forensic results of the electronics before executing an arrest. Investigators must never be in a rush to make an arrest.

As in all investigations, they may appear similar, but no two investigations are identical. Each investigation takes on a life of its own and investigators must be prepared to navigate through sudden changes. Changes that come in many forms, from one's agency to deceitful witnesses and, at times, family members. As investigations progress (slowly or fast), investigators must always stay focused and committed, and never lose sight of the result they want to achieve.

For the purpose of bringing the investigation together, let us imagine that a subject will be charged and arrested for the violent act based on facts, as well as physical and verbal evidence. While the lead investigator authors the arrest affidavit, the investigative team is responsible for summarizing their participation and ensuring that they document everything. Once this is done and the arrest affidavit has been completed, the investigation's supervisor will review the affidavit for accuracy. Once the supervisor approves the arrest affidavit, he returns it to the lead investigator for his signature. Once the investigator signs the arrest affidavit, then the supervisor signs it. Upon signing the arrest affidavit, the offender is immediately transported to the local county jail for booking and processing. Some agencies allow the media to film the offender being transported to jail. Remember to notify the victim's family of the developments leading to the arrest.

They deserve to know of the arrest (*NO DETAILS*) from the lead investigator. This will assist them with closure.

Although the lead investigator has just made an arrest with regards to their investigation, this does not mean that the investigation has ended. On the contrary, this is when the second and crucial half of the investigation begins (preparing for trial). It is important to inform the assistant state attorney assigned to the investigation that the offender was arrested and booked into the county jail for processing. With this information, the assistant state attorney can monitor when the offender will go before a judge (usually the following day) in order to establish bond (if applicable). This process is called a *bond hearing*. Generally, the lead investigator does not attend this proceeding unless circumstances dictate that they should.

Now that the initial part of the investigation has concluded, the lead investigator will brief their supervisor who will brief the command staff. A determination will be made if a press conference is necessary or if the agency will allow media outlets (if present) to film the offender. For this event, P.I.O. will be requested.

Once command staff has been briefed, it is the responsibility of the investigative supervisor to update the homicide board. Also, to ensure that the communications unit updates and removes *ALL* special messages that were disseminated to local and outside agencies regarding the particular case that resulted in an arrest. Additionally, the homicide team will meet in the criminal investigations section's conference room to debrief. During this meeting, responsibilities for follow-ups (if necessary) will be assigned and a time will be set for the 72-hour meeting. The 72-hour meeting is in furtherance of the investigation where ALL participating entities will be present to receive the final briefing and to ensure that ALL pertinent documents have been completed and submitted to the proper personnel. **Note:** The 72-hour meeting is mandatory (subject to change) and attended by the homicide team, C.I.S. commander, assistant state attorney, medical examiner, C.S.I. technicians, and any entity critical to the investigation. *This meeting is to assure that ALL information pertaining to the investigation at hand has been received and documented.* Strategies will also be discussed in an effort to solidify the case for prosecutorial purposes. Times for pre-file conferences will be set by the assistant state attorney in order to take everyone's statement regarding their role during the investigation. *It is paramount that ALL evidence has been provided to the assistant state attorney to avoid any issues pertaining to discovery violations.* This is especially important if the defense attorney waives speedy trial rules, which means that the prosecution has to be ready for trial within 21-days.

As a responsible *lead investigator* who has just dedicated countless hours, days, weeks, or months of steadfast work toward an investigation which you were not sure could be solved, but did, take time to recharge your spiritual batteries by totally disconnecting from work. Devote quality time to loved ones and make sure that you devote *'me time.'* Those who are not investigators will never understand the toll which a violent crime investigation takes on an investigator. The emotional and physical rollercoaster cannot be explained (review Mental Preparation). Remember, you have earned the rest and so has the team. Make it a point to distract yourself until such time (two-three days later) when the team unites. Those (investigative supervisors) who have had experience working difficult investigations will understand the need for such rest. Some inexperienced supervisors might have a different philosophy based on theory, not practice.

Investigators who are dedicated to their chosen profession find it difficult to disconnect because they feel they will miss something. This behavior seems normal to the perfectionist until they are able to modify it. Experience will be the teacher for such modification, just as time will be the lesson.

Once an investigator is able to make the proper adjustments, they will learn how to center themselves and not become consumed by each investigation. Extended time reliving an investigation and its horror without being able to spiritually vent (whichever way fits) will haunt any investigator for years. Recent studies have shown that investigators, after many years of confronting horrific incidents and being totally immersed in those investigations can eventually cause some form of P.T.S.D.

Now that the team is well rested, they will resume their work responsibilities and normal schedule. *One difference would be if the homicide unit or violent crimes unit have worked through a full unit rotation because of multiple investigations, then everything gets thrown out the window.* It is precisely for this reason that investigative supervisors need to monitor team assignments and rotations in order to keep them fresh. Overloaded investigators, no matter how ready they say they are, can quickly burn out if they are not careful.

Investigators and officers now need to concentrate on their administrative responsibilities, such as reviewing their field notes. These notes are to be transposed into a supplemental report which is to be submitted to the lead investigator. Once the lead investigator receives ALL supplemental reports, they will be placed in the case file after being reviewed. Additionally, these supplemental reports should contain information based on what each individual investigator or officer did during the investigation. As the supplemental reports are received, the lead investigator should check them against their notes prior to preparing the *Primary Case Supplement Report.* This report is chronologically written to depict the investigation in its entirety. Theoretically, lead investigators should have the *First Supplement Report* submitted to a supervisor for review within 30 days from when the investigation commenced. Based on the length and difficulty of each investigation is what determines when the First Supplement Report is submitted. If leads are hard to come by during an investigation and an arrest is not forthcoming, thereby extending the length (undisclosed time) of the investigation, then the *First Supplemental Report* should have *Second Supplement Report* to follow. This allows future investigators, (cold-case unit) who take over the investigation, to review the original supplemental reports. If leads are developed in the future, which enables the case to be cleared, then a follow-up supplement report (Second, Third, or Final) will be prepared. Once a case has been completely investigated and cleared, the assigned investigator's supplement report is titled, *Final Supplement Report*. All Final Supplemental Reports are submitted to the investigative supervisor for an initial review (check for grammatical, spelling, or factual errors). Once corrections (if needed) have been made, these reports will be approved by the supervisor. Upon approval, the lead investigator will enter the Final Supplemental Report into the agency's computer system as part of the electronic case management. The original hardcopy will be placed into the case file and a copy will be given to the assistant state attorney assigned to the investigation as part of discovery.

The *case file* will be reviewed by the lead investigator for completeness prior to submitting it to the investigative supervisor for approval. Once the case file has been reviewed and approved by the investigative supervisor, they will return it to the lead investigator for their signature of completion. This is followed by the investigative supervisor's signature of approval and finally the C.I.S. captain's signature. This is a check and balance to ensure that the submitted documents were properly formatted, as well as the correct case file set-up (see case-file format). Each completed case file is placed inside the vault which is assigned to the criminal investigations section. The vault is a secured location with limited access (authorized personnel only) where major case files (homicide and sexual battery files) are stored. These case files will be stored for at least 99 years or until the appeals process concludes. Cases stored inside the vault may be moved to another secured facility once the case has gone to trial and a judgment has been rendered or if there is no more storage space in the vault. If the case file is a cold case, it will be assigned to the cold case unit. It will remain inside the C.I.S. vault unless it is necessary to have it moved to the secured facility. Although the vault or secured facility can only be accessed by authorized personnel, a designated *vault custodian* will retain a log of who entered the vault and what case file was viewed or removed. Upon conclusion of reviewing or returning the specific case file, the investigator (who viewed or removed said file) will sign the vault custodian's log. This will ensure accountability for each case file in the event that the criminal investigations section gets audited by the States Department of Law Enforcement.

Now that the investigation has come to a successful conclusion, investigators feel great for having accomplished what they set out to do early on in the investigation. Their hard work, dedication, perseverance, and tenacity set them apart from others, as they were able to piece together physical evidence, combined with verbal evidence, to secure a successful outcome. Still, investigators cannot live on their laurels just because they solved one case. Investigators need to understand that they must prove themselves continuously, whether they are the lead or part of the team. **Note**: Investigators must be dependable and true stewards of their chosen profession by continuously keeping up with the latest changes in the law, new techniques, and advancements that will assist them in becoming better investigators. They should develop a habit of reviewing their cases and those of other investigators, to gain a better understanding of what strategies were used that can assist them during another investigation. Additionally, investigators can never take for granted those mentors that took time to impart knowledge onto them. Therefore, they should share with other investigators as much knowledge and advise as possible because withholding any type of information only makes them selfish and will eventually set them and others up for failure.

Remember, investigations are never over until the finding of 'guilty' is read in a court of law. Therefore, investigators must stay in constant contact with the assistant state attorney assigned to the case in order to assist them during the trial preparation, which can take up to several years.

Plenty of fieldwork and follow-ups will be required before trial and during trial. Additional information or interviews that is requested by the assistant state attorney must be conducted and are the responsibility of the lead investigator. Even though the case is in its trial phase, any additional evidence that is unearthed after an arrest has been made must be examined for its value to the case. Investigators must be willing to take on these responsibilities if they are to establish themselves as dependable and conscientious. These qualities are what separates the mediocre investigator from the elite professional.

In conclusion, it is my hope that this chapter has given aspiring investigators a better perspective of how *ALL* of the previous chapters come together to formulate an investigation. There is never a shortcut when investigating a violent crime, *ALL* shortcuts lead to disastrous endings. Each investigation must be conducted slowly and meticulously if an investigator wishes to succeed because no two investigations are exact. Investigations are fluid and investigators must be able to adapt to every change flawlessly in order to bring about a successful conclusion. Changes that occur during the course of any investigation are easily managed, so long as the lead investigator has been working the investigation methodically, *not randomly.*

FOLDER AND CASE FILE CHECKLIST

1. 911 Communications – (To include audio transmissions)
2. MGPD Event Report – (To include audio transmissions)
3. Incident Report
4. Major's Memo
5. Crime Scene Packet (Reports)
6. Property Receipts
7. Victim
    a. NCIC/FCIC
    b. Cell Orders
    c. Cell Subpoenas
    d. Any other records
8. Medical Examiner's Preliminary Report
9. Medical Examiner's Manner and Cause of Death
10. Diagram
11. Medical Examiner's Report
12. Offender
    a. NCIC/FCIC
    b. Pen Orders
    c. Cell Orders
    d. Cell Subpoenas
    e. Any other records
13. Witness
    a. NCIC/FCIC
    b. Statements
    c. Any other records
14. Crime Stoppers
15. Consents
16. Other Reports
17. First or Final Supplemental Report(s) – Lead Detective and Assisting Detectives
18. Miscellaneous
    a. news release(s)